PUZZLES, MAZES
AND
NUMBERS

Charles Snape and Heather Scott

CAMBRIDGE
UNIVERSITY PRESS

Published by the Press Sydicate of the University of Cambridge
The Pitt Building, Trumpington Street, Cambridge CB2 1RP
40 West 20th Street, New York, NY 10011-4211, USA
10 Stamford Road, Oakleigh, Melbourne 3166, Australia

First published 1995

Printed in Great Britain at the University Press, Cambridge

A catalogue record for this book is available from the British
Library

Library of Congress cataloguing in publication data
Snape, Charles.
Puzzles, mazes, and numbers / Charles Snape and Heather Scott.
    p.   cm.
1. Mathematical recreations. 2. Maze puzzles. I. Scott, Heather.
II. Title.
QA95. S519 1995
793.7'4 - dc20 94-24941 CIP

ISBN 0 521 46500 1 paperback

The authors and publishers would like to thank the following for
permission to use copyright material:
The Trustees of the British Museum, The Rhind Papyrus (page 6)
© 1994 M. C. Escher / Cordon Art - Baarn - Holland, Relativity
(page 20). All rights reserved.
© Britain on View (BTA/ETB), Carew Cross, Dyfed (page 70)
Detail of the Lindisfarne Gospels by permission of the British
Library (page 70)
© Aerofilms, Hampton Court Maze (page 102)

Design, illustration and artwork by Juliet & Charles Snape Limited

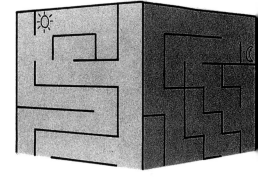

Contents

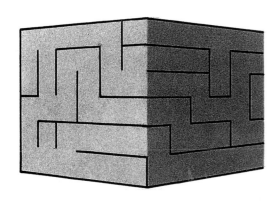

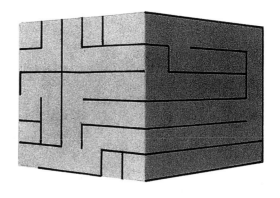

One, two and many

This shepherd of ancient times lets her goats out in the morning to graze on the surrounding hills. At night she brings them back to the compound. How can she be sure that she has brought back the same number that she let out?

When people first lived on this planet they probably did not need to count. People lived in small groups and having little or no trade within their community simply had no need of a number more than two. Even quite recently, communities which have had little contact with the outside world, have been discovered and to them everything that was more than two was 'many'.

How and why did counting start?

At some time in the distant past people settled down and began to grow crops and domesticate animals. Sometimes there were surplus stocks, and so trading began. There was therefore a need to keep some kind of accounts. This meant that some way of counting had to be invented. Did the shepherd look at her hands and think 'ah, each finger can stand for one goat'? Maybe when she got to ten – two hands – she started to use her toes, or perhaps she thought 'I could put a stone in a bag to represent each ten.' *Can you see how she might start doing simple addition and subtraction?*

It may have been her daughter or her granddaughter who came up with the big breakthrough that you could have fours or fives of different things – four goats, four apples, four trees. This is known as the fourness or fiveness. It may have been at this stage that numbers began to get names. *How would you go about giving numbers names?* In one Asian language the word for five is the same as the word for hand.

To all these generations of shepherds ten would have seemed a natural break: you could have four tens plus a hand of goats or three tens and two thumbs of bags of wheat. So how would you describe eleven? The word comes from an earlier word which means one more than ten;

similarly, twelve means two more than ten. *What would you say for three more than ten or four more than ten ..? Do you think that when you got to ten tens you might need a new name? When would you need a new number name after that?*

Names for numbers

Below are some possible names for numbers. Can you think which they stand for? Can you think of number names up to ten? A new name for one hundred?

Finger   Eyes   Feyes   Limbs

Why 10?

Probably because of the number of fingers we have, our number system is based on 10. 10 seems the natural base to use – but not quite as natural as you might think. How many seconds in a minute? Minutes in an hour? Degrees in a circle? To Ancient Babylonian priests the natural base was 60. Other civilisations developed number systems using different bases.

Pounds, shillings and pence

Until 1971, people in Britain used a money system which had three different bases. When the system was changed there was quite an outcry with people complaining that the decimals were too difficult! Pence (d) are in base 12, shillings (s) are in base 20 and pounds (£) are in base 10. *Can you do the following sums? Which system do you think is best?*

```
    £    s    d           £    s    d
   10    5   11          19    7    9
 +  3   19    7        -  8    9    6
   ■    ■    ■          ■    ■    ■

    £    s    d           £    s    d
    9   19    9          ■    ■    ■
  ×           3       3 | 10    8    6
   ■    ■    ■
```

How many?

Look at each of the pictures below, one at a time, for about a second. Make a guess at the number of bison in each picture without counting. *When do you start to guess wrongly?*

Papyrus puzzles

A quantity and a quarter of it are together 15. How much is it?

The problem above comes from one of the oldest pieces of written mathematics which has been discovered so far. It can be found on a papyrus scroll that was written, over 3500 years ago, by an Egyptian scribe called Ahmes. The scroll is called the 'Rhind Papyrus' after the antique collector, Henry Rhind, who bought it in 1858 in the Egyptian town of Luxor. Our knowledge of ancient Egyptian mathematics comes mainly from this scroll, which you can see today in the British Museum in London.

Ahmes, the writer, tells us that it is not his own work on the scroll. He explains that it comes from a scroll which was written 200 years earlier in about 1850 BC.

The scroll which was originally 30.5cm wide and 550cm long (1ft x 18ft) contains mathematical problems, exercises and puzzles. No one is sure for whom it was written; it could have been a type of text book for trainee accountants or tax collectors, or maybe even a 'text book' for school children.

Egyptian multiplication

The Rhind Papyrus shows us the way that the Egyptians, in 1650 BC, used to multiply numbers together. They used to solve problems like 15 x 16 by using a method of doubling and adding until they had the right answer:

1 x 16 or (1 lot of 16)	= 16
so 2 x 16 or (2 lots of 16)	= 32
so 4 x 16 or (4 lots of 16)	= 64
so 8 x 16 or (8 lots of 16)	=128

Altogether this comes to 15 lots of sixteen so if you add up all the answers, 15 x 16 = 240.

You may like to do the following using the Egyptian way of multiplying numbers together.

19 x 19	24 x 29	6 x 46
8 x 7	11 x 15	13 x 22

Do you think that this is a good method? Will it always work?

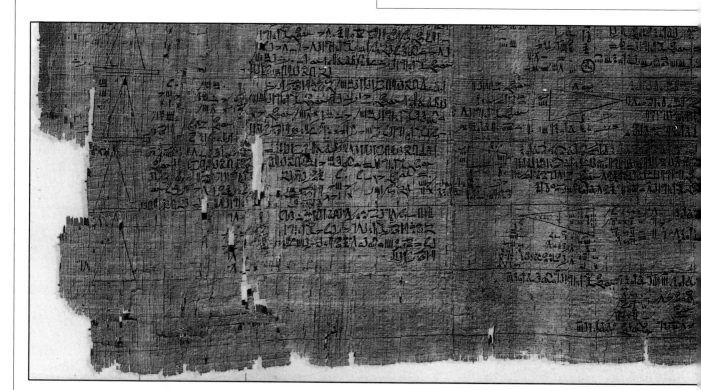

This is a section of the Rhind Papyrus. The writing on it is in hieratic script which was a development from the earlier Egyptian Hieroglyphics.

fractions which you get when you divide 2 by any odd number between 3 and 101. This is probably because it would take you a lot of time to work them out from scratch each time they were needed.

Here is the beginning of that table:

$$\frac{2}{3} = \text{ʔ}$$

$$\frac{2}{5} = \frac{1}{3} + \frac{1}{15}$$

$$\frac{2}{7} = \frac{1}{4} + \frac{1}{28}$$

Here are some examples of how the Egyptians would build up their fractions:

First find the largest unit fraction that will go into it	$\frac{5}{9} = \frac{1}{2}$ + something		(both 9 and 2 go into 18)
	$\frac{10}{18} = \frac{9}{18}$ + something		
	$\frac{5}{9} = \frac{1}{2} + \frac{1}{18}$		
	$\frac{2}{9} = \frac{1}{5}$ + something		(what number will 9 and 5 go into without any remainder?)
	$\frac{10}{45} = \frac{9}{45}$ + something		
	$\frac{2}{9} = \frac{1}{5} + \frac{1}{45}$		

Using the Egyptians' method is it possible to build up all the fractions $\frac{2}{5}$, $\frac{2}{7}$, $\frac{2}{9}$ and so on up to $\frac{2}{101}$, with just two unit fractions?

What is the minimum number of unit fractions needed to build up the fractions $\frac{3}{4}$, $\frac{3}{5}$, $\frac{3}{7}$, and so on up to $\frac{3}{101}$? Investigate with other fractions.

Problem 79

In the 79th problem on the Rhind Papyrus Ahmes poses the following question:

Seven houses each have seven cats. The seven cats each kill seven mice. Each of the mice would have eaten seven ears of wheat. Each ear of wheat would have produced seven measures of flour. How many measures of flour were saved by the cats?

Egyptian fractions

The Egyptians only used unit fractions in their mathematics. A unit fraction is one which has a '1' on the top. For example: $\frac{1}{2}$, $\frac{1}{8}$, $\frac{1}{4}$, $\frac{1}{37}$ are all 'unit' fractions. There was one exception to this rule and that was the symbol ʔ which stands for $\frac{2}{3}$. The first part of the Rhind Papyrus gives us a table of the combinations of unit fractions which are needed to make up all the

PS to problem 79

If you have worked out how many measures of flour were saved by the cats, you might like to solve the following problem in this eighteenth century nursery rhyme. You might notice the similarity with Ahmes' problem!

As I was going to St. Ives,
I met a man with seven wives.
Every wife had seven sacks.
Every sack had seven cats.
Every cat had seven kits.
Kits, cats, sacks and wives,
How many were going to St. Ives?

Theseus and the minotaur

Above is a maze pattern found at the palace of Knossos.

Below is the traditional labyrinth design. It is taken from a coin minted on Crete in about 67 BC. Designs like this have also been found all over Europe.

Part of the fascination of mazes and labyrinths is trying to trace when and where they first came into existence.

The legend of Theseus and the minotaur and the underground labyrinth is well known. Coins found at Knossos, on the island of Crete, portray labyrinth designs. Meander patterns also were meant to bring good luck and they became a favourite motif of the Romans, who used them in their mosaics.

You might like to design your own meander patterns or find out more about different meander patterns in Greek and Roman art.

seseus was the son of Aegeus, the king of Athens, and ethra, the daughter of the king of Trazen. He lived in razen while he was growing up, but when he became d enough he travelled to Athens to present himself to s father.

hen Theseus arrived in Athens, he learnt that King inos of Crete was forcing the Athenians to send seven oung men and seven young women to his island, every ne years, to be sacrificed. There they would be fed to e minotaur, a hideous creature with a bull's head and human body, who lived in the labyrinth, a vast under-round maze beneath King Minos's palace at Knossos.

seseus decided to save his fellow companions from is fate, even if this meant he would risk his life. He rsuaded his father, the king of Athens, to let him go one of the victims to be sacrificed. He sailed to Crete a ship with black sails, promising his father that he ould change the sails to white on his return if his ission was successful.

hen the seven young men and seven women arrived Crete they were taken before King Minos. There, iadne, the daughter of the king, fell in love with seseus. When the time came for Theseus to be taken the labyrinth, Ariadne secretly gave him a sword and ball of thread.

seseus tied one end of the thread at the entrance and ravelled the ball as he made his way to the centre of e labyrinth. Here he fought and defeated the inotaur. By rewinding the thread he was able to find s way out out of the labyrinth.

e news of the death of the minotaur was welcomed the people of Crete, who then turned against King inos. During this rebellion, Theseus was able to slip vay from Crete, taking Ariadne with him. On the way ck to Athens they stayed on the island of Naxos.' uring the night on Naxos some magic made Theseus rgetful. So much so that in the morning he sailed vay from the island leaving a sleeping Ariadne behind.

seseus also forgot to change the ship's sails from ack to white. As the ship approached the shores of hens, the old king thought that his son had died in e attempt to defeat the minotaur, so he threw himself to the rocks killing himself. Theseus then became e next king of Athens.

Designing key patterns

Draw a tile with exactly two halves. Make sure that the dividing line goes from one side to another opposite side.

Like this a 4 x 4 tile   or   a 5 x 4 tile...

Now repeat your tile in a row.

To turn your design into an interlocking key pattern choose one colour and colour in half of the first tile. Colour each of the other tiles in the opposite way to the one next to it.

The 5 x 4 tile would look like this.

When you are able to draw simple interlocking key patterns you may like to develop more complicated themes using larger tiles with a greater number of squares in them.

These tiles can be linked in lines or used to cover larger areas like this.

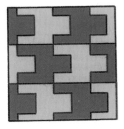

9

Church mazes

Two and a half thousand years after the legendary minotaur of Knossos met its fate, a new type of maze appeared known as the church maze. This was a flat pavement maze usually laid in a church nave or sometimes carved on a wall. Though many of them were built no one is at all sure why.

The first church mazes were constructed in the Gothic cathedrals of northern France in the twelfth century. The largest and most famous church maze is found in Chartres Cathedral. It is constructed of blue and white stones and has a diameter of about 12 metres, which is the same size as the West Rose window above it in the Cathedral.

In Italy some very small church mazes were made. One on the wall of Lucca Cathedral measures just 48.5 cm. This maze was traced by many fingers over the centuries, which eventually rubbed away the pictures of Theseus and the minotaur that had been at its centre.

Above is a plan of the maze at Chartres. The maze was made in about AD 1220.

The maze at Rheims (above) was destroyed in 1779 because of the noise the children made running around it during the services.

10

maze illustrated below no longer exists but it
thought to have been on the floor of the cathe-
l in Poitiers. You go in and out of this maze at
same place, but you could go around it many
es before you decide to come out.

reat many church mazes were built but there is
mention of them in any of the writings of their
es. It is believed that they were symbolic of the
ny twists and turns during the course of a
son's life before they could reach the next life.
he Middle Ages it was quite common for people
;o on pilgrimages. A pilgrimage is a journey to a
red place in order to make up for your sins. The
rney might take weeks or months to complete.
e centre of a church maze in France is called
usalem. This suggests that it could have been
d as a substitute for a pilgrimage to the real
usalem in the Middle East. People used to travel
maze on their knees.

Of the ten known pavement mazes in France, five
were circular, four octagonal and one was square.

At the beginning of the fourteenth century a maze was built in
Amiens Cathedral which was over 12 metres in diameter.

The plan above is of a maze in Bayeux Cathedral.

This is a plan of a maze that was in the Abbey, St Omer.

The Chartres maze has interesting properties.
The idea of four-fold symmetry is used to
represent the symbol of the Christian cross.

*By tracing around the Chartres maze what
can you find out about the symmetry of the
design?*

Crossing the river

A woman arrived at a river bank. She had with her a basket of cabbages, a goat, and a wolf. Moored by the bank was a boat which would only carry the woman and one of the other three. If she takes the cabbages the wolf will eat the goat. If she takes the wolf the goat will eat the cabbages. *How can she get herself and all three safely to the other side of the river?*

Puzzles about crossing rivers seem to have first appeared in medieval times. The one about the woman, cabbages, goat and wolf is certainly very old. Tartaglia, a sixteenth-century Italian mathematician and Lucas, the nineteenth-century French mathematician who invented the Tower of Hanoi puzzle, both worked on various forms of this type of problem. The following are some variations — can you solve them?

Mothers and daughters

Two mothers and two daughters were out walking. When they came to the river they saw that there was a shady bank on the opposite side which would be a much nicer place to picnic. Moored by the bank was a rowing boat. Unfortunately the boat was very small and could only carry the two daughters or one mother and one daughter. *What is the minimum number of crossings which they need to make so that they can all picnic on the shady bank?*

More mothers ... more daughters

You might like to pose some other problems for yourself such as what is the minimum number of crossings need for two mothers and four daughters, or three mothers and two daughters or ...

The following puzzle can be found in a book of problems published in 1612. The book *Problèmes plaisans et délectables* was written by a French mathematician Claude-Gasper Bachet.

Jealous husbands

Two wives and their husbands came to a river. Moored by the river was a rowing boat which would only hold two people at a time. However each husband is jealous and will not allow his wife to be with the other man, unless he himself is present. *How do the four people get to the other side?*

More jealous husbands

Three wives and their husbands came to the same river and used the same boat to cross it. The conditions were the same as before. *How many crossings do they need to get to the other side?*

Even more jealous husbands

If four or more wives and their husbands came to the river and were presented with the same conditions as in the previous two puzzles they would be able to cross. So would five wives and their husbands. *Can you work out how? Is there a number of couples for which it would not be possible for them to cross the river?*

Push and pull

Two engines each pulling two carriages meet on a single railway line. At the meeting point there is a spur of single line that has room for only one engine and one carriage. *How can the two trains pass each other?*

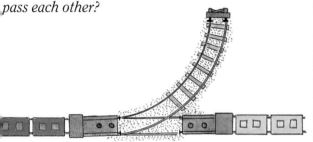

Shunting

Here is a loop of railway. The two carriages X and Y are too tall to go under the bridge B. Can the positions of the two carriages be reversed by using engine E to push or pull them?

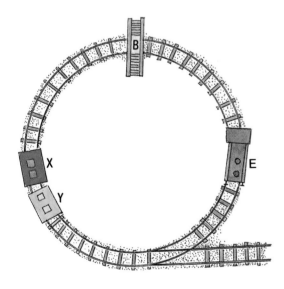

The king and his two children have been imprisoned at the top of a tall tower. Stone masons have been working on the tower and have left a pulley fixed at the top. Over the pulley runs a rope with a basket attached to either end. In the basket on the ground is a stone like the ones which were being used to build the tower. The stone weighs 35kg (75lb). The king works out that the stone can be used as a counterbalance - provided that the weight in either basket does not differ by more than 7kg (15lb). The king weighs 91kg (195lb), the princess weighs 49kg (105lb) and the prince weighs 42kg (90lb). *How can they all escape from the tower?* (They can throw the stone from the tower to the ground!)

13

Hindu number system

A million, a billion, a trillion,... we take numbers very much for granted these days. But it has not always been so.

We take it for granted that we can count beyond a million and have ways of expressing any number we choose. Yet this ability eluded scholars for thousands of years.

The key is in the use of the symbol for zero, 0, invented by the Hindus in India, probably sometime between AD 400 and 800.

The development of our modern numerals began in the Indus Valley. Evidence for this can be found carved on pillars over 2200 years old. By AD 850 all nine digits were being represented by different symbols, which weren't based on letters of an alphabet or pictograms. As the digits developed so did zero. At first it was a dot, to represent an empty column on an abacus. It was from the abacus that the Hindus also developed place value. Imaginary columns based on powers of ten represent the real columns of the abacus. Using place value, any of the digits can stand for something different. 5 can be used in 5 for five units, 50 for fifty (five tens), 500 (five hundred) and so on.

With these three developments – the nine digits, a symbol for zero and place value – came the ability to do calculations entirely with symbols, without needing an abacus.

Place value
The collection of digits above is quite meaningless, but by organising them into columns they can take on a number of meanings.

Thousands	Hundreds	Tens	Units
4	5	0	7
7	0	5	4

How many different 4-figure numbers can you make by re-arranging the digits 4507?

Powers of ten
Our number system (decimal) is based on powers of ten. When we have collected a group of ten we need to indicate this by using new columns:

Millions	Hundreds of Thousands	Tens of Thousands	Thousands	Hundreds	Tens	Units
10^6	10^5	10^4	10^3	10^2	10^1	10^0
10 × 10 × 10 × 10 × 10 × 10	10 × 10 × 10 × 10 × 10	10 × 10 × 10 × 10	10 × 10 × 10	10 × 10	10	1

This system can be developed indefinitely.

Our numerals are often called Arabic, because they came to Western Europe via the Arab civilisation. Originally the Arabs wrote out numbers word by word, even when calculating complex sums. Some mathematicians used the Ancient Greek method of representing numbers with letters but a breakthrough was made when they discovered the Indian numerals and the Hindu decimal system.

An Arab mathematician called Musa al-Khwarizmi studied the Hindu system and in AD 825 explained it in a book which, roughly translated, is called 'A Book about addition and subtraction according to the Hindu method of calculation'. However, this Arabic knowledge was not to reach Western Europe for another 300 years.

Zero sums
Is it possible to do all these sums?

100 + 0 = ■	100 ÷ 0 = ■	0 × 100 = ■
0 − 100 = ■	0 + 100 = ■	0 ÷ 100 = ■
100 × 0 = ■	100 − 0 = ■	

Liber abaci

The person credited with introducing the use of Hindu numerals into Western Europe was an Italian called Fibonacci, who lived from 1170 to 1250. In his youth he had travelled widely, visiting Africa, the Middle East and possibly India. In later years, Fibonacci became famous as a mathematician and took part in many mathematical contests that were being held at that time.

In 1202 Fibonacci published a book called *Liber abaci*. The start of *Liber abaci* demonstrates how 'with the nine Indian figures and the Arab sign 0 any number can be written'. He went on to explain how these numerals could be used to do arithmetic.

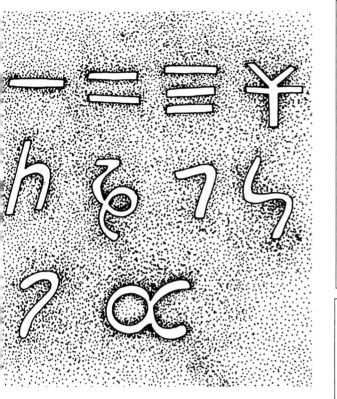

e early form of Indian numerals found in a cave in Nasik, ar Bombay, India. They are at least 1800 years old. By AD 00 these had developed in Europe into the shapes below.

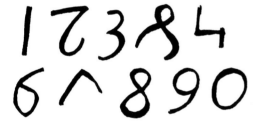

> I'm a **2**-digit Fibonacci number and I am prime. The square of my number is a **3**-digit number.

On the cards

Fibonacci introduced into Western Europe a number series that were to bear his name These are the first few Fibonacci numbers. *Can you work out how they are generated?*

1, 1, 2, 3, 5, 8, 13, ...

The number card has its back to us. It is describing the number on its front. *Can you work out what it is?* Make up some puzzles of your own.

Number series

These number series were published in 1713 in a book called *Artis Conjectandi* by Jacob Bernoulli.

Can you work out the rules for making them?

1	1	1	1	1	1	1	1	1	1	1	1
1	2	3	4	5	6	7	8	9	10	11	12
1	3	6	10	15	21	28	36	45	55	66	78
1	4	10	20	35	56	84	120	165	220	286	364
1	5	15	35	70	126	210	330	495	715	1001	1365
1	6	21	56	126	252	462	792	1287	2002	3003	4368
1	7	28	84	210	462	924	1716	3003	5005	8008	12376
1	8	36	120	330	792	1716	3432	6435	11440	19448	31824
1	9	45	165	495	1287	3003	6435	12870	24310	43758	75582
1	10	55	220	715	2002	5005	11440	24310	48620	92378	167960

Curiouser and curiouser

Alice was beginning to get very tired of sitting by her sister on the bank and of having nothing to do. Once or twice she had peeped into the book her sister was reading, but it had no pictures or conversation in it and what's the use of a book, thought Alice, without pictures or conversation?

This is how one of the most well read books in the world begins. It has now been translated into more than 46 different languages. *Alice's Adventures in Wonderland*, published in 1865, was written by Charles L. Dodgson, using the pen name Lewis Carroll.

Charles Dodgson, born in 1832, was destined to be a lover of puzzles, puns and conundrums. When he was a boy he became fascinated by puppetry and conjuring tricks. He used to entertain his family by putting on shows and he also produced magazines of puzzles and problems for his brothers and sisters. However, as a lecturer in mathematics at Oxford University he was said to be notoriously dull. Whilst at Oxford he wrote learned treatises which at the time were also thought to be boring and insignificant. Yet when Dodgson's imagination was set off on a whimsical exercise his genius shone; notably in *Alice*, which he began in 1865 as *Alice's Puzzle Book* and in *Through the Looking Glass*.

In the Wonderland book, Alice follows a white rabbit and in doing so manages to fall down a hole. As she falls down Alice begins to muse ... 'I wonder if I shall fall right through the earth? How funny it'll seem to come out among the people that walk with their heads downwards!'

A hole through the earth

At many tea and dinner parties the Victorians would amuse themselves by setting each other puzzles to solve. The problem of what would happen if someone fell down a hole right through the earth was very popular during Charles Dodgson's time. *Would that person pop out on the other side?* The following are other puzzles that were also popular at the time.

Eggs

Mrs Holly goes to market with a basket of eggs. On the way she meets Arnold the postman. She sells him half her eggs plus half an egg. Later she meets Ms Bakewell the teacher and sells her half of the remaining eggs plus half an egg. At the village pond she meets Charley, the local policewoman, to whom she sells half of the remaining eggs plus half an egg. Just before reaching the market Mrs Holly sells half of the remaining eggs plus half an egg to Denise, who delivers newspapers.

At the market, she sells half of the remaining eggs plus half an egg to Mr Early. She still has one egg in her basket. Throughout her five transactions she didn't break any eggs. *How many were in Mrs Holly's basket when she started out?*

The problem of what would happen to someone who fell down a hole through the centre of the earth is very old. Galileo came up with our current theory in the seventeenth century, but the question still puzzled the Victorians. If someone were unfortunate enough to fall down such a hole they would fall with increasing speed until they reached the centre of the earth. After this their speed would decrease. The person would not fall out of the earth on the opposite side, but would fall back towards the centre. Gradually, due to the resistance, the person would come to rest at the centre of the earth.

locks
woman has two clocks. One clock gives the
rrect time only once a year. The other is correct
ice a day. *Which is the better clock?*

More clocks
woman has two clocks. One clock lost a minute
day. The other clock didn't work at all. *Which is
e better clock?*

acks
anding by the shop door were five sacks. Sacks
nd B weighed 12kg. Sacks B and C weighed
.5kg. Sacks C and D weighed 11.5kg. Sacks D
d E weighed 8kg. Sacks A, C and E together
ighed 16kg. *What was the weight of each sack?*

The monkey and the weight
A frictionless pulley has been attached to a tower.
Around the pulley is a rope. At one end of the rope
there is a monkey, and at the other end there is a
weight. The weight exactly counterweighs the
monkey. *If the monkey began to climb the rope,
what would happen to the weight?*

An extra square

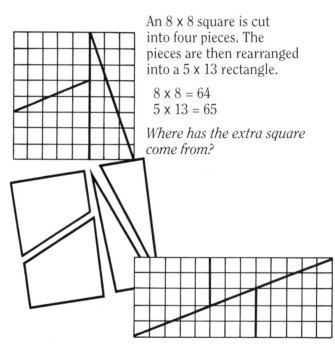

An 8 x 8 square is cut
into four pieces. The
pieces are then rearranged
into a 5 x 13 rectangle.

8 x 8 = 64
5 x 13 = 65

*Where has the extra square
come from?*

Further escape
The problem on page 13, 'Escape from the
tower', was probably invented by Lewis Carroll.
Almost certainly the following addition to the
puzzle is his.
Besides his two children the king also has a pig at
the top of the tower which weighs 28kg (60lb), a
dog which weighs 21kg (45lb) and a cat which
weighs 14kg (30lb). There is an extra limitation
that there must be one human at the top and
bottom of the tower to put the animals in and out
of the basket. *How can all six escape?*

Sam Loyd

In a box are fifteen square tablets and there is a space for a sixteenth. The square tablets are numbered 1 to 15, in order, except for 14 and 15 which have been reversed as in the diagram. The tablets can slide horizontally or vertically one space at a time. The puzzle is to rearrange the tablets by sliding , so that all the numbers are in the correct order.

Sam Loyd offered a prize of $1000 to the person who could solve his 'fourteen-fifteen' puzzle. No one claimed the prize – the puzzle was impossible!

Sam Loyd (1841-1911) is perhaps America's greatest creator of puzzles. During his lifetime he is reputed to have made more than a million dollars from his inventive mind. He was devising puzzles before he was in his teens. When he was only seventeen he thought up the famous Donkey Puzzle. P.T.Barnum, owner of *The Greatest Show on Earth*, paid Sam Loyd ten thousand dollars to use it to advertise his show.

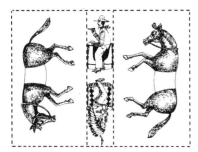

Trace this drawing. Cut along the dotted lines. *How can you fit the three pieces together so that both riders are correctly riding a horse?*

Below is one of Sam Loyd's most popular puzzles.

How many pieces of various sizes can you cut this pie into with six straight cuts?

Inventing a puzzle

Sam Loyd was once asked what the mental process was for inventing puzzles. He replied that he wasn't quite sure but that the puzzles were all based on mathematics. He then went on to describe how one puzzle had come into his mind.

Sam was in the office of a pen manufacturer discussing with the owner the idea of offering some pens as prizes for his puzzles. During the course of a conversation, Sam persuaded the manufacturer to spend one thousand dollars on advertising in a puzzle magazine that he was starting up. Suddenly a puzzle popped into his head. Sam drew nine eggs and then said... 'What is the least number of straight lines needed to connect all nine eggs? The lines may pass through an egg twice and may cross.' The pen manufacturer thought it looked easy so Sam said, 'If you can solve it within an hour, I'll give you your thousand dollars of advertising free.' Alas, the manufacturer was unable to solve it.

O O O

O O O

O O O

What is the least number of straight lines needed to join the nine eggs? Lines may cross and may go through an egg twice.

Henry Ernest Dudeney

Henry Ernest Dudeney was born in the English village of Mayfield in 1857. He became as famous in England for his puzzles as Sam Loyd was in America. The two were producing puzzles at much the same time. Although it is unlikely that Dudeney and Loyd ever met, they did write to each other and exchange ideas. The following are a small selection of the many puzzles invented by Dudeney.

The Merchant's puzzle

One morning when they were on the road, the Knight and the Squire, who were riding beside the Merchant, reminded him that he had not yet propounded the puzzle that he owed the company. He thereupon said, "Be it so. Here then is a riddle in numbers that I will set before this merry company when next we do make a halt. There be thirty of us in all riding over the common this morn. Truly we may ride one and one, in what they do call single file, or in a column of twos, or threes, or fives, or sixes, or tens, or fifteens or all thirty in a row. In no other way may we ride so that there be no lack of equal number in the rows. Now a party of pilgrims were able to thus ride in as many as sixty-four ways. Prithee tell me how many there must perforce have been in the company."

The Merchant clearly required the smallest number of persons that could so ride in the sixty-four ways.

Dividing three numbers

Find a number which will divide the numbers 480 608, 508 811 and 723 217 to leave exactly the same remainder in each case.

The dispatch rider

A dispatch rider has to ride his horse from the rear of an army column to the general at the front. The army, which is forty miles long, advances forty miles whilst the rider gallops from the rear to the front. *How far has the dispatch rider travelled, if he also rides back to the rear again?*

Triangle numbers

In his book *Amusements in Mathematics*, first published in 1917, Dudeney looks at triangle numbers...

These are numbers which can be represented by counters arranged as shown to form triangles. You may like to draw the next triangle numbers in the sequence ...

Dudeney also points out some other things about triangle numbers. For example, choose any number, times it by itself and add the original number. Halve the result and you will always get a triangle number. You might like to try it with some numbers...

5 + (5 x 5) = 30 then half of 30 is 15
15 is a triangle number!

He also said that if you choose any number you will find that it is either a triangle number, or you will be able to make it by adding together two or three triangle numbers.

You might like to see if this works with a few numbers...

11 is made up of 10 + 1   (two triangle numbers)
12 is made up of 10 + 1 + 1 (three triangle numbers)
          or   6 + 6   (two triangle numbers)
13 is made up of 10 + 3   (two triangle numbers)

What else can you find out about triangle numbers yourself?

Puzzling reality

Two-dimensional (2-D) mazes can be difficult to transverse but when an extra dimension is added they become even more so...

A maze can be made three-dimensional (3-D) in a variety of ways. Escher, a Dutch artist, drew many unreal patterns which cannot really be made in three dimensions. They are illusions created by showing 3-D images in a 2-D picture.

Above: Escher's fascinating impossible 3-D design invites the viewer to follow the little people on their never-ending path.

Above: Did you notice the cubes at the beginning of the book? The three diagrams represent the six sides on a maze drawn on a cube. *Can you find a route from the sun to the moon?*

Below: The maze at Longleat, Warminster, in Wiltshire is 3-D because there are six overpass bridges and a viewing tower included in the layout. It was designed by Greg Bright and 16 000 English yew trees were used to create the 2.72 km of pathways. It covers an area of about 6000 square metres, making it the largest maze of this type in the world. There are two sections to the maze: a fairly straightforward part, which takes approximately half an hour to complete, and a more challenging second section, which can take an hour or more to solve.

3-D maze

You can design your own unreal 3-D pathway or maze by using dotty isometric paper. Below are some examples to show what might be done.

Moving

The fox and the goose chase

A group of people make themselves into a moving maze. Standing in a grid they must stretch out their arms so that their fingers touch. Three more people are to act; one as the fox, one as the goose and one as the wind. The fox tries to catch the goose, who must try to escape. Both are allowed to run up and down the avenues in the grid, but not go under or pass through any of the arms that are outstretched. The wind chooses when to blow the whistle, which tells everyone in the grid to turn 90° clockwise. This makes it very hard for the fox to catch the goose!

Moving crates

The storeroom is almost full of heavy crates. *How can the storewoman get the shaded crate to the doorway?* She can only move one crate at a time, horizontally or vertically, into the next empty square of the grid. She cannot stack one crate on top of another. *What is the smallest number of moves the storewoman can do it in?*

Investigate what happens in different sizes of floor grids, with more or fewer squares but still only one space free.

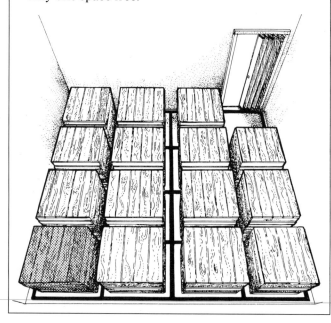

Moving pyramids

Fifteen pyramids sit on a board made up of 4 by 4 squares. The pyramids can only make a knight's move onto an empty space. A knight's move in the game of chess is two squares forward then one square at a right angle either to the left or right. *How many moves does it take for the shaded pyramid to reach the top right-hand corner? What happens in different sized grids?*

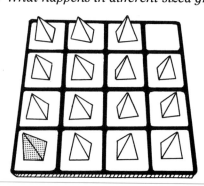

Sliding cups and saucers

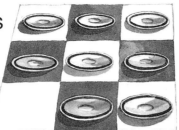

The cups and saucers shown on the board can move one space horizontally or vertically per move. They can also jump over another cup or saucer into a vacant square.

How many moves does it take to exchange the positions of the cups with the saucers?

Investigate for different sized grids.

The strange interview

Five candidates have been called up for an interview. It was decided to keep the candidates separate from each other so that they can't give away any of the questions. When they arrived they were each put into a different room as shown below. Unfortunately the secretary realised that he had made a mistake. Raji should have been in room 6 and Helen in room 3. The others could be in any room. *How will the secretary move the candidates around so that no two people will meet each other and in the quickest possible time, in other words, the fewest number of moves, so that his mistake won't be discovered?*

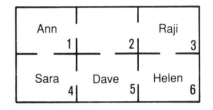

Bridge-it

David Gale invented a game for two players called Bridge-it in 1958. A board is drawn up on squared paper as shown, colouring the dots on alternate rows in two colours. The players decide which colour to be, and only join up dots of their own colour.

Playing alternately, each player is allowed to draw a line connecting two dots which must be next to each other. Lines are not allowed to cross other lines. The winner is the person who connects up a line of his or her colour dots going from one side of the board to the opposite side.

The board can be any size but it must have an equal number of dots of each colour. Use squared paper to help you draw up the grid.

This game is in play. The person who chose black dots joins the dots with straight lines and the person who chose the white dots joins them up with squiggly lines. It is the straight line's turn next. *Will black dots or white win?*

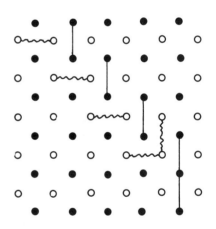

The game of Hex

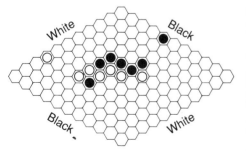

This game involves two players trying to find a pathway across a board at the same time as trying to prevent their opponents from doing so. Players choose their colour, using counters to show where they have been. Two opposite sides of the board belong to white, and the other two sides to black.

The object of the game is to form a continuous line of your own pieces joining your two sides of the board. The line does not have to be straight, but must link. Corner hexagons belong to either side. Turns are taken alternately, placing a piece on any hexagon. Once a piece is put on the board it cannot be moved.

It's black's turn next. *Who is likely to find a pathway across first?*

Play the game. *Are Bridge-it and Hex the same?*

Really big numbers

The Ancient Greek way of writing numbers was based on letters of the alphabet. This made working with them very difficult and most arithmetic was carried out on an abacus. Working with letters also made the writing down of big numbers very clumsy. The Greeks had a word 'myriad' which meant 10 000, but to most people this was such a large number that they thought of it as meaning 'uncountable'.

'How many grains of sand are there in the world?' This was the question that the Greek mathematician, Archimedes (287–212 BC), posed in a book called *The Sand Reckoner*. 'How many grains of sand on a beach?' '...a million? ...a billion? ...a googol?' To most people at that time, the only way they could see to do this would be to sit on the beach and count each grain one at a time. This would take a very long time, and when they got past 10 000 they had no way of writing it down.

How many grains of sand are there in the world?

Too many to count ...?

In his book, Archimedes described a way to count the sand by making bigger and bigger units. Start by counting how many grains of sand would equal a grain of wheat, then work out how much wheat would fit in sack, how many sacks would fit in a boat, how many boats would fit on a beach and so on. The method he used to represent these bigger and bigger numbers was to have myriads of myriads (10 000 × 10 000) and myriads of that number and so on. In this way Archimedes was able to describe numbers that would have a one followed by millions of noughts.

How many grains?

Twenty grains of sand take up as much space as a grain of wheat. A beach is 500 metres long, 10 metres wide and 2 metres deep. *Can you work how many grains of sand the beach contains?* (You will first need to estimate how many grains of wheat there are in, say, 1 cubic cm.)

Powering up numbers

Another way of writing four is 2^2. This means 2×2. The small two means multiply the number by itself. $3^2 = 3 \times 3$, $4^2 = 4 \times 4$. The result of multiplying a number by itself is called a square number.

Another way of writing eight is 2^3.
This means $2 \times 2 \times 2$. When a number is multiplied by itself in this way it is called a cube number.

Another way of writing sixteen is 2^4.
This means $2 \times 2 \times 2 \times 2$. The small number is called an index. When a number is written with an index we say that the number is to the power of that index. For example:

4^5 is 4 to the power of 5, which is 1024.

Can you work these out?

$5^4 \quad 6^2 \quad 7^3 \quad 4^6 \quad 2^{10}$

Which of these pairs of numbers is the biggest?

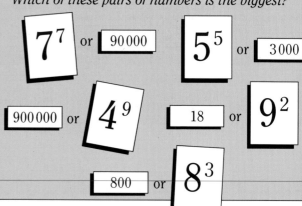

7^7 or 90 000 $\qquad$ 5^5 or 3 000

900 000 or 4^9 $\qquad$ 18 or 9^2

800 or 8^3

Sky high numbers

Approximate distance in km from the Sun

Mercury	Venus	Jupiter	Saturn
58 000 000	110 000 000	770 000 000	1 427 000 000
Uranus	Neptune	Pluto	
2 800 000 000	4 400 000 000	5 900 000 000	

Altair (White star)	150 000 000 000 000
Sirius (White star)	82 000 000 000 000
Procyon (Yellow star)	104 000 000 000 000
Beta Centauri (Blue-white star, as bright as 10 000 Suns)	
	3 700 000 000 000 000

Above are some approximate distances from the Sun to some heavenly bodies. *Which is the third furthest from the Sun?* Astronomers and other scientists working with very large numbers need to have a less cumbersome way of writing them down. The method they use is called 'standard form'.

Standard form is based on powers of 10. So, for example, $10 \times 10 \times 10$ is written 10^3 (10 to the power of 3). $10 \times 10 \times 10 \times 10 \times 10$ would be written as 10^5. The distance from Mars to the Sun is approximately 200 000 000 km, which in standard form is 2×10^8. This is how it is worked out:

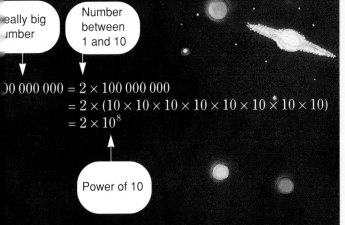

really big number → Number between 1 and 10 →

$$200 000 000 = 2 \times 100 000 000$$
$$= 2 \times (10 \times 10 \times 10 \times 10 \times 10 \times 10 \times 10 \times 10)$$
$$= 2 \times 10^8$$

Power of 10

The distance Earth to the Sun is about 150 000 000 km, which in standard form is 1.5×10^8.

$$150 000 000 = 1.5 \times 100 000 000$$
$$= 1.5 \times (10 \times 10 \times 10 \times 10 \times 10 \times 10 \times 10 \times 10)$$
$$= 1.5 \times 10^8$$

Can you write the distances from the Sun to the heavenly bodies in standard form? Can you write the number of grains of sand on the beach in standard form?

Googol

For many centuries an old French word, million (probably from an older Italian word, *mille*, which meant 1000) proved adequate to describe the biggest numbers but with the increase in trade, the rise in money supply and inflation, new variants had to be coined. Thus we have billions, trillions and octillions. Each meant an almost uncountable number when first used. But what do you do when you want a name for an incredibly large number? The answer for one American mathematician was to go home and ask his young nephew, who came up with the word 'googol'. It had no particular meaning but the googol is now used in most languages to describe an incredibly large number – such as 1 followed by 100 noughts.

$$10^{100} = 1\,0000000000000000000000$$
$$0000000000000000000000$$
$$0000000000000000000000$$
$$0000000000000000000000$$
$$0000000000000000000000$$

Base two

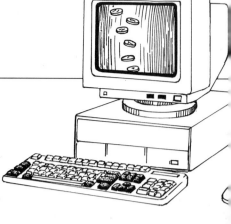

There are 1100100 pennies in a pound!
This is how a computer would count them.

We do our calculations in the decimal system, which uses base ten. Computers work with the binary system and use base two. In base two all numbers can be represented using 0 and 1. In base 10, each new column is the next power of ten; in base 2, each new column is the next power of 2.

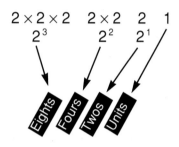

$$2 \times 2 \times 2 \quad 2 \times 2 \quad 2 \quad 1$$
$$2^3 \qquad\qquad 2^2 \quad 2^1$$

Eights | Fours | Twos | Units

The number 47 would be written 101111.

Thirty twos | Sixteens | Eights | Fours | Twos | Units

1 0 1 1 1 1

$$32 + 0 + 8 + 4 + 2 + 1 = 47$$

The number 117 would be written 1110111.

Sixty fours | Thirty twos | Sixteens | Eights | Fours | Twos | Units

1 1 1 0 1 1 1

$$64 + 32 + 16 + 0 + 4 + 2 + 1 = 117$$

Can you translate these binary numbers into decimal numbers?

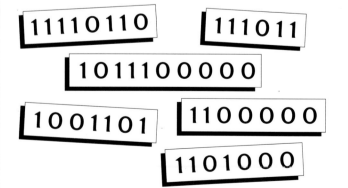

11110110		111011
1011100000	
1001101	1100000
	1101000

Which base?

Base 2 is the most commonly used base other than 10. But other bases can be used. Each pair of dice add up to seven in base 10 but they have been put into different number bases. *Can you work out which base has been used for each pair?*

How to add in base two

```
  4  2  1
  1  0  1
- 1  1  1
```

```
  8  4  2  1
     1  0  1
 +   1  1  1
 ─────────────
   1  1  0  0
```

When you get 2 ones in a column you add a one to the next column. When you get 2 ones in the highest value column you make a new column. *Can you do the following additions?*

1100 + 10001

100101 + 101100

10000 + 10110

110000 + 1010110

How to subtract in base two

```
  4  2  1
  1  1  0
- 1  0  1
```

```
  8  4  2  1
     1  1  0
 -   1  0  1  ←  You take 1
 ─────────────    from the 2's
           1      column
```

Can you do the following subtractions?

111 - 11

101110 - 100010

11101 - 1011

10010 - 1001

Puzzling?

New job

At noon John tells four friends that he has got a new job. By 12.05 pm the four friends have each given the information to a further four people. So 20 people now know that John has a new job. By 12.10 pm all 20 people have each told another four people.

If the information is passed on in this way every five minutes, how many people will know that John has got a new job by 1.00 pm?

Doubling

A very special water lily doubles its size every day. After 30 days it will completely cover a circular lake. *How much of the lake would it cover after 15 days?*

Millions more

Assuming that there is a new set of parents every 25 years, this family tree proves that there were millions more people alive a thousand years ago than there are now. *Or does it?*

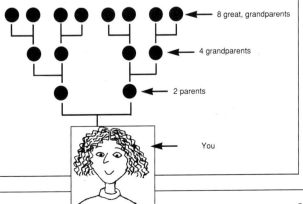

8 great, grandparents

4 grandparents

2 parents

You

27

Problems of Babylon

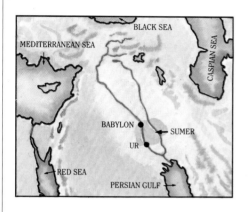

The Babylonians lived in the Mesopotamian valley in the Middle East. Their civilisation lasted for about 1400 years between 2000 BC and 600 BC.

We are able to find out about the type of mathematics which the Babylonians did because they used to write in 'cuneiform script' by pressing triangular shaped wedges into clay tablets.
These cuneiform tablets were then baked until they were hard to give a permanent record of their work, which we are able to decipher and read today.

The following is an old Babylonian problem.

Silver and sisters
There are eight sisters who have to share $1\frac{2}{3}$ minas of silver between them. Each sister in turn receives more than the previous sister and the difference between the quantities that each successive sister receives is the same. If the second sister gets six shekels, what is the common difference?

A talent is worth 60 minas

A mina is worth 60 shekels

A shekel is worth 60 grains

Babylonian Number System
The Babylonian number system is interesting for many reasons. They used 60 as a base, probably because it was useful for astronomical calculations and the practical problems concerned with weights and measures. This base 60 system has certainly stood the test of time as it is still frequently used today. *How many seconds are there in one minute? How many minutes in one hour? How many degrees are there in one full turn?*

| 1 | 2 | 3 | 4 | 5 | 6 | 7 | 8 | 9 | 10 |

Using the system the number 90 would be represented by

1 lot of 60 and 3 lots of 10 makes 90.

Can you match the questions with the answers?

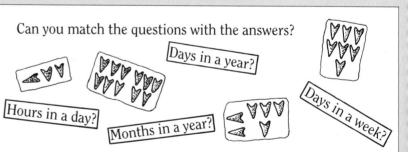

Days in a year?

Hours in a day?

Months in a year?

Days in a week?

Babylonian square

What is the length of the side of the square? If the area of a squa less its side is

14 lots of 60 and 3 lots of 10 (which equals 870 in our decimal system).

In the Babylonian system the value of the wedge depended upon its position. Because there was no symbol for zero this created a problem with knowing exactly how much the number was worth. For example ...

does ▽ ▽▽ ▽▽ stand for

3 lots of $(60)^2$ and 2 lots of 60 which would make 10920 as we know it?

▽▽▽ ▽▽

or does it stand for 3 lots of 60 and 2 which makes 182 as we know it?

Because the Babylonians also used the same symbols for fractions it could also stand for 3 lots of 1 and 2 lots of $\frac{1}{60}$ which makes $3\frac{1}{30}$ as we know it. With no zero you needed to be able to understand the problem being posed so that you would know how large the numbers should be.

Measuring land
The Babylonians used practical methods to measure land. They would cut up shapes and turn them into rectangles.

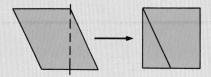

To turn a parallelogram into a rectangle you only need to make one cut along the dotted line, as shown. *How many cuts would you need to turn each of the following shapes into rectangles?*

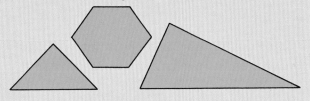

Babylonian hand
A quarter of the width of an object and one length, added together make 7 hands. Also, the length and the width added together make 10 hands. *What are the length and the width?*

Investigating reciprocals
Ancient cuneiform tablets have been found which show tables of numbers constructed by the Babylonian mathematicians. One of the most fascinating to investigate is the table of reciprocal numbers. Here is the beginning of this table:

This stands for 2

This stands for 3

This stands for 30 sixtieths ($\frac{30}{60}$) which is what you get when you divide 1 by 2 ($\frac{1}{2}$) in base 60.

This stands for 20 sixtieths which is what you get when you divide 1 by 3 in base 60.

In our number system (base 10) the reciprocal of 3 is $\frac{1}{3}$ or 1 divided by 3. In the Babylonian system the

reciprocal of 3 is still $\frac{1}{3}$ but you have to do the division in base 60.

$$\overset{0,20}{3\overline{)1,^60}}$$

3 into 1 won't go. So the 1 is changed to 60 sixtieths. 3 into 60 goes 20 times.

How would you carry on the Babylonian table of reciprocals?

Are all the numbers easy to work out?

What differences are there between reciprocals in our decimal system (base 10) and the Babylonian sexigesimal system (base 60)?

Puzzling paths

The nature of a maze is to find a path from a beginning to
an end through the puzzle of dead ends or repeated routes.
There may be only one way to travel through the maze but
this single path twists and turns many times before
reaching its final goal. Many games are based upon the
idea of finding the single path or finding the shortest
route.

The Icosian game

The Icosian game was invented by Sir William Rowan
Hamilton. You have to find your way around the board
so that you visit every vertex (corner) once and once
only. (You do not have to travel along every path.)
When you have found one route try to find others. *How
many different routes are there?*

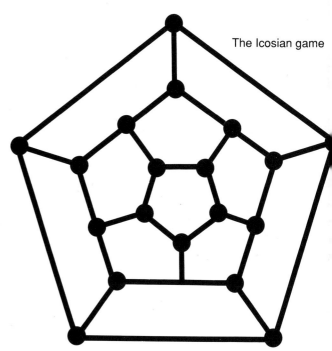

The Icosian game

The Icosian game is based upon three pentagons inside
each other. The problem below is based upon three
heptagons inside each other, and the moves are made
by jumping over vertices (corners).

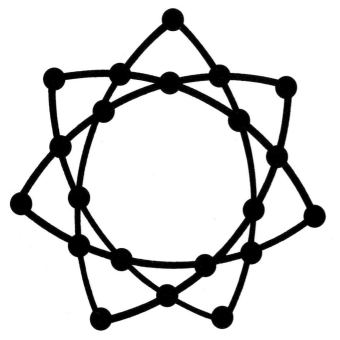

Place a counter in any position to start the game.
Moving with the curve of the lines, place a counter on
every other vertex that you visit. You may not change
direction in mid-move, nor go back on yourself. You
may jump over a vertex with a counter on it but you
may not land on a vertex already occupied by a counter.

Can counters be placed on all the vertices in this way?

Can every vertex but one be covered in this way?

mazing Sam Loyd

m Loyd was a famous creator of puzzles at the
ginning of this century. Many of his mathematical
zzles are about finding routes which visit the
iximum number of places, or take the shortest
ssible path.

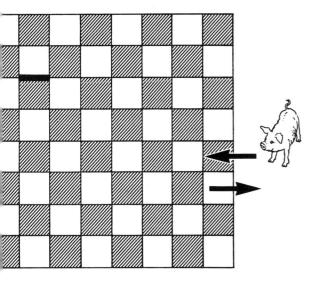

at and mice

other puzzle involves a cat catching mice, which are
iced on the vertices, by following the given paths.
ike a copy of the grid shown opposite. Place counters
each vertex and choose your pathway. As you land on
ertex you remove the counter. *What is the minimum
nber of moves you need to make to remove all the
unters?*

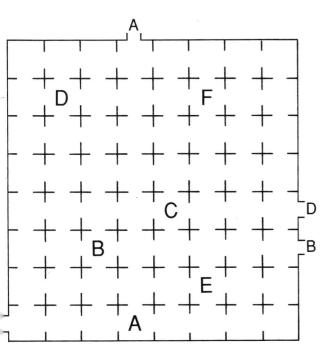

Pig in the garden

In the 'pig in the garden' problem, a pig enters the
garden at the grey square marked with an arrow. It then
visits each square in the garden once and once only. The
pig may only move in straight horizontal or vertical
lines and can make 90° turns. The pig is not allowed to
cross the black gate. Having visited every square, the pig
leaves by the white square marked with an arrow. *Can
you find a route that visits every square?*

Sam Loyd gives a solution where the pig makes twenty
90° turns. *Is twenty the smallest number of 90° turns
that the puzzle can be done in?*

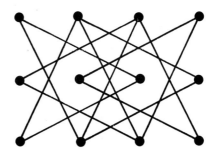

Tower of London

Sam Loyd's 'Tower of London' puzzle has a further twist
to it. Five people must find their own route without
meeting any of the others – or going over the same path
as anyone else. This is how Sam Loyd sets the puzzle:

Five guards are represented on the plan of the tower by
the letters A,B,C,D and E. Promptly at the firing of a
gun, which denotes the setting of the sun, guard A
marches out by exit A, B exits at B, C exits at C, D exits
at D, while E marches from his present position to cell
F. The problem is to discover how the five guards can
make these five marches without any one man crossing
the line of march of another. In other words, no more
than one line of march is permitted through any one
cell.

Can you do it?

Chessboard problems

A chessboard is a square plane which has been divided into 64 squares by straight lines at right angles. The earliest boards which have been found were not chequered (black and white in alternate squares) ... this was a much later development which was introduced to help the players see the moves more easily. For example, the bishop which is only allowed to move along diagonal lines, keeps to the same colour which makes it easy to see which squares he might attack.

Why isn't the answer to the question above 64? If you start with a smaller sized board (a 3 x 3 board) and look carefully you will be able to see different sized squares.

First of all it has 9 small squares ...
Then, 4 different overlapping larger squares...
Then there is also the outside square to add on.

How many squares on a chessboard? No, not 64 ... nor 65 ...

Try thinking about a 4 x 4 board next.

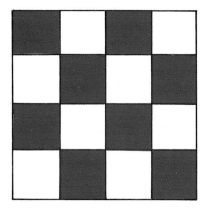

When you have worked out how many squares there ar on a chessboard (an 8 x 8 board), try to explain how yc could work out how many squares there were on any sized square board.

32

...how many different ways can you divide a
...essboard into two equal parts of identical shape just
...cutting along the lines between the squares?

...hequerboard divisions

...u can look at this problem in a similar way to the
...vious one. *How many different ways can you divide*
...x 2 board into two equal parts? (Ways are only
...unted as different if you cannot reflect or reverse the
...ces to get a way that you have already counted.) The
...swer is, one way, by cutting straight down the
...ddle.

...w think about a 3 x 3 board. *What is the*
...blem with all odd x odd boards?

...re are three ways of dividing a 4 x 4 board.

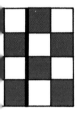 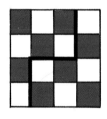 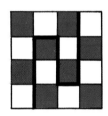

...fact there are six different ways of dividing a 4 x 4
...rd into two equal halves. *Can you find the other*
...ee ways? How many ways are there for a 6 x 6
...rd? ... an 8 x 8 board? ...

...dd x odd board divisions

...u can tackle the odd x odd board problem by blocking
... the centre square. Now the board has an even
...mber of squares so you will be able to divide it into
... equal halves. Remember that you may only cut
...ng the lines. A 3 x 3 board has only one solution.
...at about a 5 x 5 board, and a 7 x 7 board and so
...

Lions and crowns

The women above is confronted with a cutting
problem. She needs to cut the square piece of
material into four equal parts and it is essential
that each part should contain a lion and a crown.
She also insists that the cuts can only be made
along the lines drawn on the material. *Can you*
think of a way to do this so that each piece of
material is exactly the same shape and size?

The golden chessboard

Below is an illustration of a golden chessboard.
Set into the board are four red rubies. *Can you*
divide this precious board into four equal parts
so that each part is the same shape and size and
also contains a ruby?

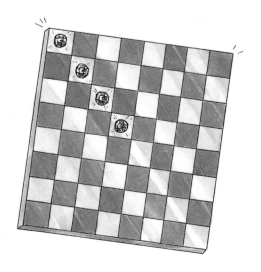

33

Problem pieces

It has been shown that there are at least 197 299 ways of playing the first four moves in a game of chess – that is with each player making two moves. There are 71 782 different positions possible after playing the first four moves – 16 556 are possible when the players only move the pawns.

The eight queen problem

One of the classic problems connected with the chessboard is finding a way to put eight queens on the board so that no queen can take any other queen. There are 92 different ways in which this can be done. One of the ways is shown below. *Can you find any of the other 91 ways?*

Another classic problem is to put five queens on a chessboard so that every square is 'commanded' by at least one queen. There are 4860 solutions to this problem. *How many different ones can you find? Can you find a way to place the five queens so that no queen is able to take any other queen?*

Guarini's problem

One of the oldest problems in Europe connected with the chessboard was posed in 1512. On a board with nine squares, the two white knights have to change places with the two black knights (using knight's moves only). *What is the least number of moves which you need to do this?*

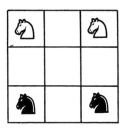

Routes

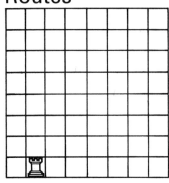

The rook starts in the square next to the bottom left. It must visit every square, once and once only, and finish in the top right hand square. *Can you find a route?*

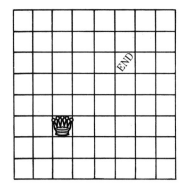

Move the queen to the end position in fifteen moves, visiting every square once and once only, so that she never crosses her own track.

Getting started

Using one set of chess pieces and one chessboard, what is the maximum number of different ways of placing the pieces for the beginning of a game?

Weights and measures

Three robbers stole a jar containing 24 ounces of valuable balsam. Whilst making their escape they came upon a seller of containers, from whom they purchased three empty jars. When they reached their hiding place they decided to share out the balsam but found that their jars would only hold 5, 11 and 13 ounces respectively. *How could the valuable liquid be divided equally amongst the three by only using the four jars available?*

This problem is the first printed puzzle involving measuring liquids. It was posed by a sixteenth century mathematician, Niccola Fontana, who is more often referred to as Tartaglia. *Can you find a way to share the balsam which takes fewer pourings than your first try? Have you found how to do it with the least number of pourings?*

4 litres
You have a five-litre jug and a three-litre jug and a supply of water. *How can you measure exactly 4 litres?* (You are allowed to throw water away!)

8 litres
On the table are three jugs. The largest is full and contains 8 litres of wine. The other jugs are empty but can hold 5 litres and 3 litres respectively. The problem is to divide the wine so that there are 4 litres of wine in the eight-litre jug and 4 litres of wine in the five-litre jug. *What is the least number of pourings you need to do this if:*
(a) you first pour wine into the five-litre jug?
(b) you first pour wine into the three-litre jug?

12 litres
Change the sizes of the jugs to 12, 7 and 5 litres. Starting with a full twelve litre jug of wine, *how many pourings do you need so that there are 6 litres in each of the two larger jugs?*

24 litres
This time start with a 24 litre jug full of wine and two empty jugs of 15 and 9 litre size. *How many pourings are needed now, if you want 12 litres in each of the two larger jugs?*

Double orange
A litre carton of orange juice has all of its dimensions doubled. *How much orange juice would it hold?*

35

Pythagorean triples and triangles

The Ancient Egyptians used a rope with 13 equally spaced knots in it to mark out square corners of fields when they measured out their land. This was done regularly as the farmers were taxed on the size of their fertile fields along the banks of the Nile which were often flooded, and bits of them would be swept away. A similar system was used in China for land surveying.

The (3, 4, 5) triangle is a right-angled triangle. If you square each of the numbers you will find that the two smaller square numbers add together to make the larger square number:

3   4   5
9   16   25
9 + 16 = 25

Groups of three numbers with this property are called *Pythagorean triples*, after the Greek mathematician Pythagoras, who lived in the 6th century BC.

The Hindus in India also needed to use right angles. In addition to the (3, 4, 5) triangle which the Egyptians discovered they found that the following right-angled triangles had the same property:

(12, 16, 20)   (8, 15, 17)   (12, 35, 37)
(15, 20, 25)   (5, 12, 13)   (15, 36, 39)

Some of these can be made by using the (3, 4, 5) triangle and multiplying each number in the triple by another number. For example:

```
     3    4    5
   × 4  × 4  × 4
   = 12   16   20
```

Some of the triples are *primitive triples*, for example (3, 4, 5), because the numbers cannot be found from another set of triples by multiplying. *Which of the Hindu triples are primitive? Which have been made by multiplying a primitive triple by a common multiplier*

Here are the first 12 primitive triples: (3, 4, 5) (5, 12, 13) (8, 15, 17) (7, 24, 25) (20, 21, 29) (12, 35, 37) (9, 40, 41) (28, 45, 53) (11, 60, 61) (16, 63, 65) (33, 56, 65) (48, 55, 73). There are 158 primitive triples where the three numbers add up to less than 1000. *How many can you find?*

Diophantus and the early Greeks used formulas to generate Pythagorean triples. Choose two numbers m and n and put the numbers into each of the following formulas:

To find the first answer do $m^2 - n^2$
To find the second answer do $2mn$
To find the third answer do $m^2 + n^2$

By using these formulas it is possible to find some interesting patterns in Pythagorean triples.

● Use pairs of consecutive numbers for m and n to generate Pythagorean triples – *what do all the triples have in common?*

● Use pairs of triangle numbers for m and n to generate Pythagorean triples – *what do all the triples have in common?*

Making Pythagorean puzzles

Square to square
Draw 2 squares accurately next to each other. Label each of the corners of the squares.

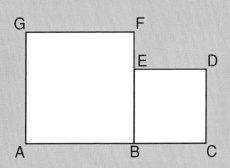

Put another point (H) on the diagram so that the distance from A to H is exactly the same length as the side of the smaller square (B to C).

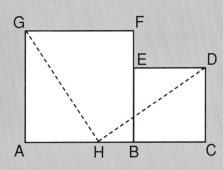

Now draw a line from G to H and from H to D.

Cut out each of the five pieces you now have and put them together to make one larger square.

Perigal's dissection
A mathematician, Perigal, showed in 1873 that it is possible to use three cuts to divide two squares into five pieces which can always be re-formed into one square.

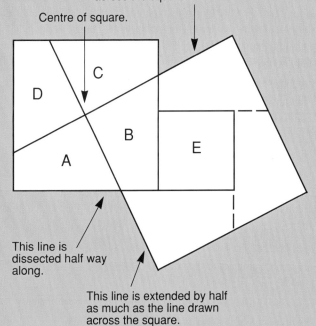

This line is extended by half as much as the line drawn across the square.

Centre of square.

This line is dissected half way along.

This line is extended by half as much as the line drawn across the square.

Cut pieces A, C, D and slide them into place on the larger square.

Triangles to spirals
In the centre of a page draw a right-angled triangle with two sides exactly one unit long (say 1.5cm).

Draw a new right-angled triangle on the hypotenuse of the first triangle keeping the outside side one unit long – 1.5cm.

Continue this process. *What shape will you create?*

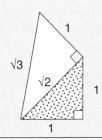

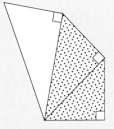

Counting on

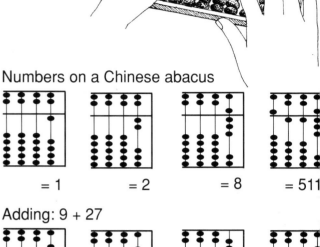

Abacus

Although no one knows who invented the abacus, or when, it is likely that it developed independently in different countries.

It is thought that the word abacus comes from a Hebrew word meaning dust. In Ancient Israel numbers were represented by the 20 letters of their alphabet plus an extra four characters. As with the Greek system, this made manipulating numbers – addition, subtraction, multiplication and division – almost impossible, so it was only used for official records of the government or religious authorities. Ordinary people used a much simpler method of covering a table with sand and using marks such as dots to do calculations. When a calculation was completed the sand would be brushed ready for a new one.

The Romans used a table with grooves carved on it. A Roman merchant would place small stones, called *calculi*, in the grooves. These stones would be moved up and down in the grooves to do calculations.

The form of abacus that we are most familiar with probably developed in China. The Chinese put balls on wires and hung them in a frame. As in the Roman system, the balls were moved up and down on the wires to do calculations. This is the system still in use in some parts of the world; various countries developed their own kind of abacus. Three are shown here.

Numbers on a Chinese abacus

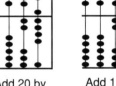

= 1   = 2   = 8   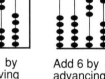= 511

Adding: 9 + 27

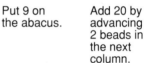

Put 9 on the abacus.

Add 20 by advancing 2 beads in the next column.

Add 1 by removing 4 and lowering 5.

Add 6 by advancing 10, removing 5 advancing

Read off the answer: 36

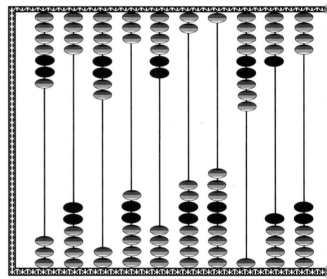

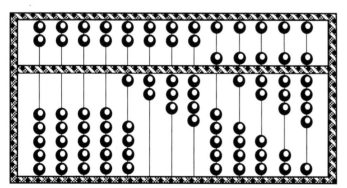

Above: Chinese abacus. Right: Russian abacus.
Below: Japanese abacus. One abacus shows 7483621954,

the others show 7946.8723457694 and 123456789. *Can you work out which abacus shows which number?*

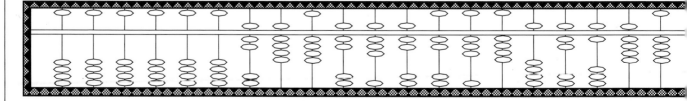

1	2	3	4	5	6	7	8	9	Indicator strip
1	2	3	4	5	6	7	8	9	I
2	4	6	8	1/0	1/2	1/4	1/6	1/8	II
3	6	9	1/2	1/5	1/8	2/1	2/4	2/7	III
4	8	1/2	1/6	2/0	2/4	2/8	3/2	3/6	IV
5	1/0	1/5	2/0	2/5	3/0	3/5	4/0	4/5	V
6	1/2	1/8	2/4	3/0	3/6	4/2	4/8	5/4	VI
7	1/4	2/1	2/8	3/5	4/2	4/9	5/6	6/3	VII
8	1/6	2/4	3/2	4/0	4/8	5/6	6/4	7/2	VIII
9	1/8	2/7	3/6	4/5	5/4	6/3	7/2	8/1	IX

Napier's bones

Before the electronic calculator, almost every mathematics student would have used a set of logarithms. This was a book of tables which allowed a student to multiply very large numbers together by doing simple addition. These sets of logarithms were devised by a Scottish mathematician called John Napier (1550 –1617). Another set of tables, also devised by Napier and known as Napier's bones, is shown opposite. The bones were used to do calculations that involved multiplying and dividing large numbers.

The example here shows how to use Napier's bones to multiply:

1548×43

The bones are used to do the four multiplications: 8×43, 40×43, 500×43 and 1000×43. The answers to these calculations are then added together to obtain the final answer.

4	3	I
8	6	II
1/2	9	III
1/6	1/2	IV
2/0	1/5	V
2/4	1/8	VI
2/8	2/1	VII
3/2	2/4	VIII
3/6	2/7	IX

Make a copy of the table and cut the columns into strips. Put the 4 and 3 strips together so that the top row reads '43', with the indicator strip beside them as shown.

Use row VIII to calculate 8×43. Add the numbers that fall within the diagonal lines.

3/2	2/4	VIII

$8 \times 43 = 3 \quad 4 \quad 4$

Similarly, use row IV to calculate 4×43 and add a nought so that you have 40×43.

1/6	1/2	IV

$40 \times 43 = 1 \quad 7 \quad 2 \quad 0$

Row V will give you 500×43 and row I will give you 1000×43. Add the answers together:

```
        344
       1720
      21500
      43000
1548 × 43 = 66564
```

See if you can do these multiplications using Napier's bones.

2496 x 382   **11243 x 5432**

84 x 716   **9875 x 3143**   **635 x 4157**

A number puzzle

2	1	9
4	3	8
6	5	7

There are many ways to arrange the digits 1 to 9 so that the first and second rows sum to the total of the third row. *How many ways can you find?*

Networks

The puzzle above is based on a problem which was tackled by an eighteenth-century mathematician called Leonhard Euler. He proved that it was impossible to travel over all seven bridges of Königsberg once and once only. Euler's discovery led the way for a new branch of mathematics called *network theory*.

Euler did not need to visit Königsberg to show that a journey around the town, crossing all the bridges, was impossible without retracing one's path. Instead he drew a map which showed that Königsberg was divided into four separate parts by a river.

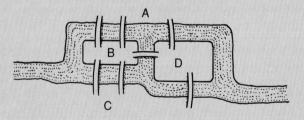

By placing a point in each of the four parts and joining

them up with lines he got the following diagram:

This diagram, called a *network,* shows all the routes that could be taken.

Network names

A point in a network is called a *node*. A line joining a point to another point, or a point to itself, is called a *branch*.

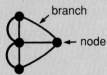

If all the branches in a network can be passed along once and once only in a single journey, then the network is said to be *traversable*.

There are seven bridges in this Chinese garden. *Can you find a route which crosses all the bridges once and once only? What happens if you use one of the sets of stepping stones?...or both sets?*

ven node, odd node

node at which an even number of branches meet is lled an even node. The *order* of a node is the number branches that meet at it.

 even node of order 2   even node of order 4

node at which an odd number of branches meet is lled an odd node.

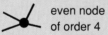 odd node of order 3   odd node of order 5

ler discovered that the number of odd nodes in a twork will tell you whether a network is or is not versable.

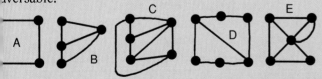

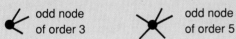

ove are some networks. *Which of them are traversle?* Draw some networks of your own. Make some of em quite complicated. Which are traversable? Keep a

record of your results as you go along using a table like the one below. You can start at any of the nodes in a network.

Network	Number of even nodes	Number of odd nodes	Is it transversable ?
A	4	0	YES
B			
C			

Important discoveries

Euler's researches into networks led to two discoveries:

1. A network that only contains even nodes is always traversable.

2. A network that contains more than a certain number of odd nodes is not traversable.

Look at your table. *Do your results agree with these two discoveries? What is the maximum number of odd nodes that can be in a network before it stops being traversable?*

Numbers for Greeks

It is often thought that the study of mathematics originated in Ancient Greece. But, like all civilisations, the Greeks borrowed and learnt from other civilisations. What the Greeks gave us was the idea that mathematics could be studied for its own sake.

Unity

The number one was called *unity* by the Greeks. It was probably the Greeks who first divided numbers into odd and even. The Greek mathematicians, especially those who were followers of Pythagoras, began to look for meaning in numbers. It was the Greeks who first began the search for prime numbers. A prime number is a number that has only itself and unity as factors. A factor is a number that can be divided into another number with no remainder.

Perfect numbers

One type of number the Greeks found they called a *perfect number*. A perfect number is one where all its factors except itself sum to that number. The smallest perfect number is 6.

$$1 + 2 + 3 = 6$$

The next smallest is 28. Check it out!

The Greeks found only four perfect numbers between 1 and 10 000. *Can you find the other two?*

The perfect numbers 6 and 28 convinced the Pythagoreans that numbers in themselves had some secret meaning.

Imperfect numbers

An *imperfect number* is one where the sum of its factors is either lesser or greater than the number itself.

If the sum of the factors is less than the number itself then it is called *deficient*.

If the sum of the factors is more than the number then it is called *abundant*.

Can you classify these numbers into deficient and abundant imperfect numbers?

35, 42, 56, 64, 70, 84, 99, 102, 112, 155

Amicable numbers

Another group of numbers the Greeks discovered are called *amicable*. Amicable numbers are a pair of numbers whose factors sum to each other.

The smallest pair of amicable numbers is 220 and 284. we add the factors of 220 we get:

$$1 + 2 + 4 + 5 + 10 + 11 + 20 + 22 + 44 + 55 + 110 = 28$$

and if we sum the factors of 284 we get:

$$1 + 2 + 4 + 71 + 142 = 220$$

1184 and 1210 are another pair of amicable numbers. Check them out.

The story of amicable numbers so far

All our knowledge of Greek mathematics comes to us very much second hand. There are no surviving manuscripts and the copies that exist are copies of copi. However, we are fairly certain that Pythagoras would have known the lowest pair of amicable numbers, but w have no way of knowing if he knew of any others.

For about 1200 years after the Greeks no one seems to have come up with any more until another pair were fou in 1635 by the French mathematician Pierre de Fermat. His pair were 17 296 and 18 416. At about the same time another French mathematician, René Descartes, discovered another pair, 9 363 584 and 9 437 056.

It was to be another 100 years before any more amicabl numbers turned up. The Swiss mathematician Euler published a list of 60 amicable numbers; unfortunately two of these prove not to be so!

It wasn't until 1830 that another pair was found by a French mathematician called Legendre. 37 years later, the mathematical world was astonished when a 16-year old Italian boy discovered another pair. What was even more astonishing was that this pair was the second lowest and had been overlooked by Western mathematicians for over 300 years. (This was the amicable pair 1184 and 1210.)

More than 600 amicable pairs are known today, many o which contain over 30 digits.

he Ancient Greeks adopted two methods of recording numbers hat made doing sums almost impossible.

ttica symbols

e first method of recording numbers used by the
eeks was Attica, named after the area around Athens.
was not too dissimilar to the Egyptian way of writing
mbers at that time. Our knowledge of the Ancient
eek Attica numbers comes mainly from fragments of
ttery found many years after the Ancient Greek
ilisation ceased. Between about 500 BC and 100 BC,
iting, especially on things like pots, could be written
t to right, right to left or one line left to right and the
xt line right to left. Above on the right is a table of
e Greek Attica numbers.

I	Γ	Δ	Ρ	H	Ρ	X
1	5	10	50	100	500	1000

n you work out what numbers are represented by
ese Attica symbol groupings shown on bits of broken
ttery?

Ancient Greek puzzle

A bowl of olives was divided between
six people. Argos got one-third, Beta
got one-eighth, Cicely got a quarter
and Delphi got a fifth. Elysium got ten
olives and Furi got only one olive. *How many*
olives were there in the bowl originally?

nic numbers

the century before the birth of Christ, Attica had
en replaced by another way of writing numbers,
own as Ionic. The Greeks adopted a method
veloped by the Ancient Hebrews, which used letters of
e alphabet to represent numbers. Not only did this
ake calculations with numbers very difficult, it also
eant they had to invent new symbols because their
phabet contained only 24 letters. The Greeks worked
base 10.

n you complete the 10 × 10 multiplication table
posite? The Greek letter Σ represented 200. Can you
ake a multiplication table up to 15 × 15?

	A	B	Γ	Δ	E	F	Z	H	Θ	I	
A	A	B	Γ	Δ	E	F	Z	H	Θ	I	A
B		Δ	F	H	I	IB				K	B
Γ										Λ	Γ
Δ										M	Δ
E					KE					N	E
F										Ξ	F
Z										O	Z
H									OB	Π	H
Θ										q	Θ
I										P	I

The Chinese Triangle

The number triangle above appeared in 1303 in a Chinese book by Chu Shih Chieh, called *The Precious Mirror of the Fair Elements*. The symbols represent numbers. By looking at the first few rows of the triangle you should be able to see how the triangle is made and what number each of the Chinese symbols represents. It would then be possible to carry on with the triangle for many more rows.

There are many interesting number patterns within this triangle. They can be found by looking along different lines of numbers as shown opposite.

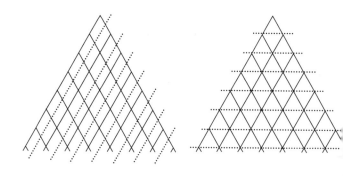

is also possible to create geometric patterns using the [tri]angle as a basis for determining different colouring [ar]rangements. The pattern below is created by fitting [to]gether six of the number triangles which have been [ma]de by using the modulo 3 system for addition, as [de]scribed underneath.

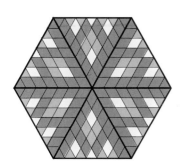

The triangle below is created using addition in modulo 3. Once the numbers have been found each number is given a different colour. The coloured triangle is then used to make the hexagon.

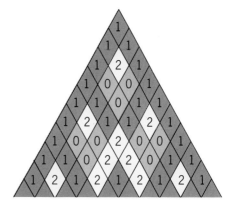

[In] modulo 3 you use a clock with 0, 1 and 2 on the face. [On]ly the digits 0, 1 and 2 are used. For example:

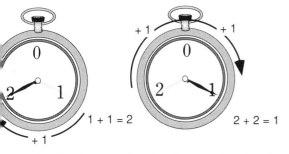

$$1 + 1 = 2 \qquad 2 + 2 = 1$$

:
$$0 + 1 = 1 \qquad 1 + 1 = 2 \qquad 2 + 1 = 0$$
$$0 + 2 = 2 \qquad 1 + 2 = 0 \qquad 2 + 2 = 1$$

Different patterns can be created by using different modulo systems for adding together the numbers. It would also be possible to use different starting numbers in the top of the pattern, or use a different generating rule to create the numbers.
Investigate these different triangles.

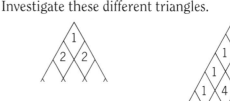

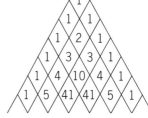

The Indian Triangle

The triangle also appeared in India in the 10th century. It was known as the *meruprastara* and was drawn out by a person called Halayudha. The *meruprastara* was used to work out the number of ways short and long sounds could be combined together in poetic rhythms of different lengths.

You can make up your own music in a similar way. Instead of thinking about a long and short sound the following idea is based on either making a sound or having a rest. Decide whether you will make your sound with your voice or with a musical instrument. Decide how long you want your line to be and then work out how many different combinations there would be for putting the sounds and the rests together. For example, if your line is going to be 3 beats long then you could arrange your sounds as follows:

beat	beat	beat
beat	beat	rest
beat	rest	beat
rest	beat	beat

rest	rest	rest
rest	rest	beat
rest	beat	rest
beat	rest	rest

If a group of you play several lines together repeatedly you can make some interesting rhythms. For example, person A could play beat rest beat, beat rest beat, beat rest beat, at the same time as person B plays rest beat beat, rest beat beat, rest beat beat, and so on. You could create more variations by using different instruments.

Create different rhythms by looking at the combinations possible in a 4-beat line. *Can you see how the meruprastara helped with calculating how many different combinations there were?*

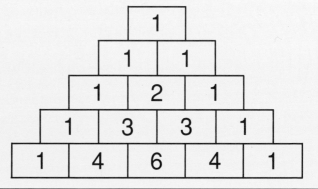

Inside or outside

In the branch of mathematics called *topology* a circle is called 'a simple closed curve' which divides a flat surface into an inside and an outside.

The diagram below shows a simple closed curve which is said to be 'topologically' the same as a circle. *Can you say which dot is inside the curve and which is outside?*

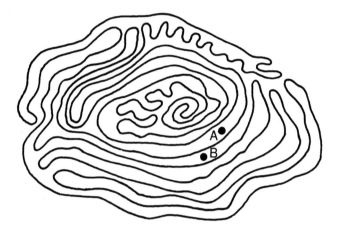

To get from the inside of a circle to the outside it is necessary to cross the curve as in the diagram below...

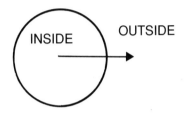

...but in the following diagram if you cross into A, are you inside or outside?

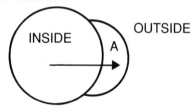

Below is a Jordan curve. It is also a simple closed curve and so it is topologically the same as a circle. An easy way to find out if a point is inside or outside a Jordon curve is to count the number of times the curve is crossed by drawing a line from the point to a place obviously outside the curve. *If the number of lines is an odd number, is the point inside or outside the curve?* Find out the rule using the Jordan curve below.

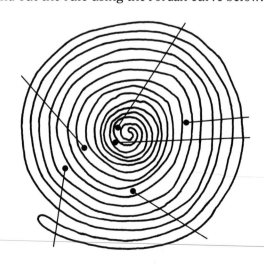

Topological trick 1

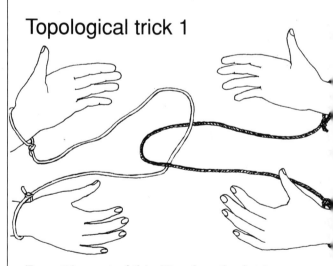

Try getting out of this. Tie a length of string around a friend's wrists. Do the same to yourself but before you tie the string to the second wrist, loop your string through your friend's. Now try to separate yourselves from each other without undoing any knot or cutting any string.

eformations

sphere made of a soft squashable material, such as
ay, can be shaped into a cube, flattened to make a
ate, or pressed to make a jar. Shapes like this which
n be made from each other without breaking or
ning are said to be topologically the same. A sphere
nnot be made into a doughnut shape without break-
g a hole into it. So a sphere and a torus (a doughnut
ape) are not topologically the same. But if you start
th a doughnut, it can be flattened, pulled and pushed
form a cup. The doughnut and the cup are
pologically the same. The changing of a shape into
other is called a *deformation*.

Genus

e can describe 3-D objects by looking at their genus.

sphere has a genus 0 because there are 0 holes in it.
doughnut has genus 1 because there is 1 hole in it.

you do cut through 3-D objects it is possible to get
fferent results.

you make one cut in a
here you will always get
o parts each with a genus
0.

you make one cut through
doughnut you could get
e object of genus 1 and
e object of genus 0 or
o objects of genus 0.

*an you work out the genus of the objects on the
ght?* You are allowed to transform the objects
pologically but you are not allowed to cut them or
ar them or make any new holes in them.

vestigate what happens with objects of different
nus. Investigate what happens with objects which
u cut two, three, four times and so on.

Topological trick 2

In the illustration below a loop of string is placed
around a friend's thumbs. The string is threaded
through a ring. Is it possible to remove the ring
without lifting the string from the friends
thumbs? Read on...

Place your left forefinger over both strands on
the left of the ring.

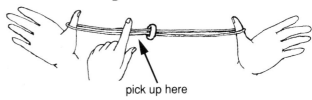

pick up here

With your right hand pick up the strand of string
nearest to you at the point shown and loop it
over the friend's thumb that is on your left.

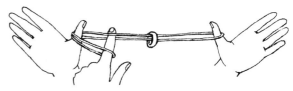

Still holding your left forefinger in position pick
up the strand of string nearest to you on the
right of the ring. Loop it over the same thumb of
the friend (the thumb on your left!). There are
now two loops over that thumb. Remove your left
forefinger slowly and the ring will be released.

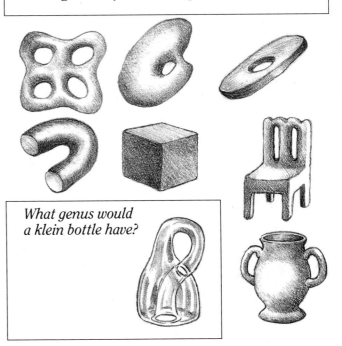

*What genus would
a klein bottle have?*

Ways with numbers

In some mazes, when you come to a junction you have to make a decision about which way to go. Depending on what you decide, there may be other choices ... all of which give rise to a variety of different routes you could take in trying to reach the goal in the maze.

Imagine that you live in a town where the streets are arranged as a rectangular grid.

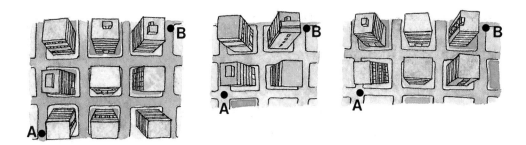

Investigate the number of different routes you could take to get from A (bottom left) to B (top right) for each of the above towns of different sizes.

Smallest sum ... biggest sum

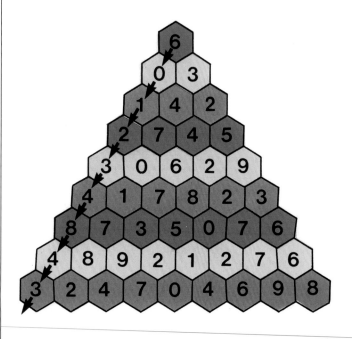

The route shown on the number maze adds up to 31. *Can you find a route that adds up to 41?* You must sta[r]t at the top hexagon and finish in one of the hexagons in the bottom row. You may go down or across but not u[p].

Can you find the route which adds up to the smallest total? Can you find a route which adds up to the bigge[st] total?

Trace the grid and make up some puzzles of your own. Try using different types of numbers such as very large numbers, decimals, fractions...

...then try to solve your own maze.

ays in ways out

w many different routes can you find through this
ze? Start at the top row and end at the bottom.
ain you can only move across or down. There are
ny ways to get from the top row to the bottom row
this maze. To do so follow sets of special numbers,
example square numbers or multiples of numbers.
ich set of numbers gives a route which goes
ough the most hexagons? Which set of numbers
es a route which goes through the least number of
xagons?

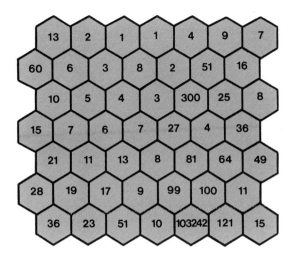

ogue dice maze

ings in this maze do not add up. Find a route along the rogue dice from the top row to the bottom.

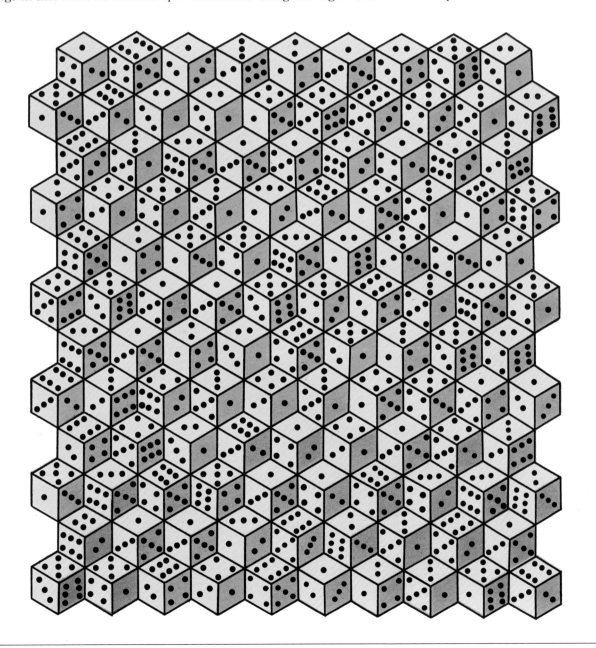

Paradoxes of Zeno

Zeno of Elea lived about 450 BC. He put forward 'arguments', which although they seemed logically sound, confused the mind and seemed to defy common sense. *How would you argue against Zeno's paradoxes?*

Achilles and the tortoise

Achilles and a tortoise have a race. Achilles allows the tortoise to have a head start. They both start at the same time, but ... for every amount that Achilles moves forward, the tortoise must move forward as well. So when Achilles manages to reach the place where the tortoise was, the tortoise will have already moved on from there. This will continue indefinitely, so in this way Achilles will never be able to catch up with the tortoise.

The arrow

Another of Zeno's paradoxes states that if you imagine an arrow flying through the air, then at any one particular instant the arrow must be in one particular place in space. (Especially as it cannot be in two places at once!) So if it is in this space at this instant, then it cannot be moving at all. This argument also holds for all other instants! In fact, you are just imagining that the arrow is moving.

Diophantine problems

The life of Diophantus

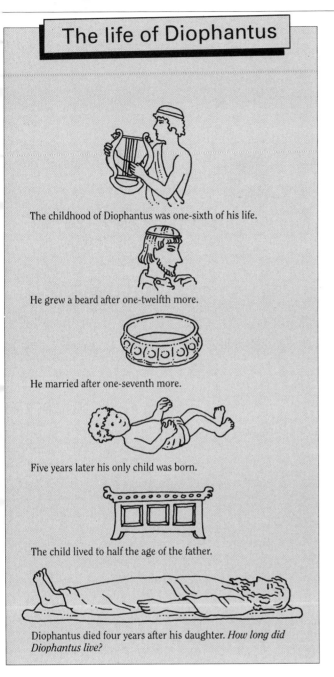

The childhood of Diophantus was one-sixth of his life.

He grew a beard after one-twelfth more.

He married after one-seventh more.

Five years later his only child was born.

The child lived to half the age of the father.

Diophantus died four years after his daughter. *How long did Diophantus live?*

Solving the problem

Diophantus of Alexandria was a Greek mathematician who lived in about 300 AD. He is best known for his collection of 189 problems and their solutions which he wrote in a book called *Arithmetica*. By using a form of algebra that was a mixture of words and symbols he was able to solve indeterminate (problems which have more than one solution,) and determinate equations (problems with only one solution). The problem above is said to have been written by a pupil of Diophantus. *Can you work out how long Diophantus lived?*

One solution

Below are some determinate equations-that is they have just one solution. Can you solve them? The first two are quite easy but the third is hard.

> Find two numbers whose sum is 20 *and* the sum of their squares is 208.

> Find two numbers whose sum is ten *and* the sum of their cubes is 370.

> A farmer goes to market with 100 krona to spend. Cows cost 10 krona each, pigs cost 3 krona each and sheep cost half a krona each. The farmer buys from the cattle dealer, the pig dealer and the sheep dealer. He spends exactly 100 krona and buys exactly 100 animals. How many of each animal does he buy?

Many solutions

The problem of Diophantus' life is a determinate equation and would probably not have interested Diophantus very much. Diphantus' fame lies in his invention of symbols to help him look logically at some mathematical problems and the solving of indeterminate equations (which are usually called Diophantine Equations). The following is an example:

If Sally has two more than three times as many pennies as Paula, how many does Sally have?

This problem has an infinite number of solutions ... if Paula had 5 pennies then Sally would have 17 pennies, if Paula had 6 pennies then Sally would have 20 pennies, if Paula had 7 pennies ...
Because there are an indeterminate number of solutions the best way to show the answer is in an algebraic form.

$x = 3y + 2$

Can you find a solution to the following Diophantine equation? Duncan is two years more than five times older than Eric. *How old is Duncan?*

A Diophantine day

I've got a problem about going to a shop in France. I found it in an old algebra text book which was used by children in 1855.

What's the problem then?

First you need to know that one French Louis is worth 20 francs and 25 francs are worth one British Pound...

Got that.

Imagine that you only have one pound coins in your pocket and the French shopkeeper only has Louis coins in her till. How can you pay for something that costs 45 francs, simply by paying with British pounds and getting French Louis coins back from the shopkeeper?

I like that problem because you can think about what would happen for different amounts of money. And which amounts of money are possible and which aren't.

Try something that cost £2.25

AFTER A MORNING IN TOWN THE FIVE WERE RETURNING HOME... THE PUZZLING CONTINUED...

...I've been looking at the prices of sweets in one of the shops.
I found that 3 small bars of chocolate and 1 bar of toffee cost as much as 1 packet of wine gums.
If 1 small bar of chocolate, 2 bars of toffee and 3 packets of wine gums cost £1.25 how much did each thing cost?

Whilst you are figuring that one out... remember the wool I went to buy? Well I bought 2 different sorts. One sort cost 40p per ball and the other cost 55p per ball. I spent £15 altogether... so how many of each sort did I buy?

I knew today was going to be special. I think I call it a Diophantine Day.

WHY DID MELANIE CALL IT A DIOPHANTINE DAY?

53

A page of π

Finding π (approximately 3.142)

How do you 'measure' π*?* Use a tape measure or a piece of string, as described below. Find a number of different-sized circular objects such as tin cans, plates, waste bin.

Use a ruler to measure the diameter of each of the objects and write the results down.

	DIAMETER
CAN	
BIN	
PLATE	
BIG CAN	

Now measure around the circular object or find some string and wind it once around the object.

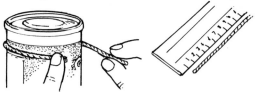

Unwind but keep careful hold of where the string meets. Measure the length of the string with your ruler and write down the results in a table.

	DIAMETER	CIRCUMFERENCE	C÷D
CAN			
BIN			
PLATE			
BIG CAN			

Now divide the circumference of each object by its diameter. Look at the results – *what do you notice?*

Find some more circular objects. Measure their diameter. *Can you predict their circumference?* You can check your prediction by measuring.

Pi (π) has puzzled mathematicians throughout the age It is a special type of irrational number called a *transcendental* number. This means that, unlike all decimal fractions, it will continue without ever repeating in a pattern and without ever coming to an end. Therefore π can never be written down exactly.

Throughout history, mathematicians have spent time trying to calculate π to an ever-increasing number of decimal places. The Ancient Egyptians, Hebrews and early Chinese used the value 3.

More accurate values of π than 3 were needed when machinery based on the wheel began to come into use. For example, Archimedes, an Ancient Greek mathematician, invented a method for launching ships using cogs and his invention of an irrigation pump wa based on the rotation of a screw.

Archimedes drew regular polygons inside circles (inscribed) and outside circles (circumscribed) to get approximations of π. The more sides the polygon had the closer would be Archimedes' approximation.

Archimedes' method

Keep the radius of the circle equal to 1 and then the area of the circle, which is πr^2, will be equal to π.

The area of the circle is bigger than the inscribed triangle but smaller than the circumscribed triangle.

The area of the circle is bigger than the inscribed square but smaller than the circumscribed square.

The area of the circle is bigger than the inscribed pentagon but smaller than the circumscribed pentagon.

using regular polygons with 96 sides, Archimedes ⟩wed that π was larger than $3\frac{10}{71}$ but smaller than $3\frac{1}{7}$.

⟩hough mathematicians have calculated π to a large ⟩mber of places it is very unlikely that the number will ⟩r need to be used with that degree of accuracy. As ⟩non Newcomb, an American astronomer and ⟩thematician, wrote:

⟩n decimal places are sufficient to give the
⟩cumference of the Earth to the fraction of an inch,
⟩d thirty decimal places would give the circumference
⟩the whole visible universe to a quantity
⟩perceptible with the most powerful telescope.

⟩ccurs in other places. It is used by actuaries in a ⟩rmula to calculate the number of people left alive in a ⟩en group of people after a certain number of years.

Mathematicians have also calculated π by creating formulae which will give an approximation to π. As the series grows, the answer gets closer to π.

Lord Brouncker (1620–1684)

$$\pi = \cfrac{4}{1 + \cfrac{1^2}{2 + \cfrac{3^2}{2 + \cfrac{5^2}{2 + 7^2}}}}$$
$$\cdots$$

John Wallis (1616–1703)

$$\frac{\pi}{2} = \frac{2}{1} \times \frac{2}{3} \times \frac{4}{3} \times \frac{4}{5} \times \frac{6}{5} \times \frac{6}{7} \times \frac{8}{7} \times \frac{8}{9} \times \cdots$$

Leibniz (1646–1716)

$$\frac{\pi}{4} = 1 - \frac{1}{3} + \frac{1}{5} - \frac{1}{7} + \frac{1}{9} - \frac{1}{11} + \frac{1}{13} - \frac{1}{15} + \cdots$$

Matching π

The following experiment will give you a number which is approximately equal to π.

Use some headless matches. On a piece of paper draw some parallel lines which are double the distance apart as the matches are long. Hold the matchsticks about 30 cm above the paper and drop them one by one. Count the number of matches that have either touched or crossed a line.

When you have finished making the drops do the following calculation:

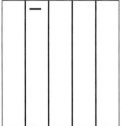

(Total number of matches dropped)
÷ (Total number of matches crossing or touching line)

Matchsticks must be half the length of the distance between the lines.

The more times you drop the matches the more likely it is that your result will be close to π.

Some puzzling circles

Floating island
A family of seals inhabits this circular island of ice. After a family row they agree to divide the ice island into two identical pieces with the same number of seals on each part as they are positioned now. *How did they do it?*

A magic circle
A magician placed 10 penguins into a magic circle as below. She then drew 3 more magic circles inside the large one so that if none of the penguins crossed any of the magic lines they would each have their own compartments. *Where did she draw her circles?*

Inventing mazes

Above: the thick line is the true route and the thinner lines are the false paths. Below: the grid has been traced over to form the walls of the maze.

...he way to create your own maze is to start with a
...idded paper. It could be squares or as in this example,
...xagons. Trace a complicated path from one side to
...e other. Then have false paths leading off. Make sure
that paths go through every hexagon. When you have
done this, trace over the gridded paper. The lines of the
grid which have not been crossed by any of the paths
become the walls of the maze.

...ove and below: the same maze is given different treatments. Invent some mazes of your own. Use different grids and dotty
...pers.

Arabian mathematics

Lattice multiplication

The Arabs developed a way of multiplying called the 'lattice' method. This is how it works.

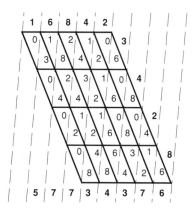

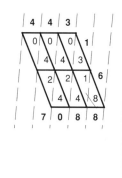

Lay out the numbers to be multiplied along the top and down the right-hand side. You make small multiplications to fill the cells. *Can you see how?* To get the product of the two numbers you add the numbers on the diagonal – carrying over when necessary. The number of cells needed depends on the lengths of the numbers that are being multiplied together. Trace over the grids and try to do these multiplications.

8964 × 73   **56482 × 16**

7286 × 253   **764 × 764**

Casting out nines

This is a method that was used in India to check that an answer to a large multiplication was correct. This is how it works for $16\,842 \times 3428 = 57\,734\,376$.

Sum, separately, all the digits in the two numbers multiplied and divide by 9.
$1 + 6 + 8 + 4 + 2 = 21 \div 9 = 2$ r3
$3 + 4 + 2 + 8 = 17 \div 9 = 1$ r8   (r means remainder)

Multiply the remainders together and then add the digits of the answer.
$3 \times 8 = 24$ $2 + 4 = 6$

Now sum the digits of the answer to the multiplication and divide by 9.
$5 + 7 + 7 + 3 + 4 + 3 + 7 + 6 = 42 \div 9 = 4$ r6

If the two remainders are the same, 6 in this case, then the multiplication is probably correct. *(Can you think why it might not be?)* If the two answers are not the same then your multiplication is definitely wrong.

Mathematics is always developing

The development of mathematics has taken place over the centuries and each civilisation across the world has played an important part in its development. New ideas are discovered by mathematicians and ideas from previou times and different civilisations are explored and developed further. The Arabians made contributions to many aspects of mathematics, including the theory of numbers, the development of algebra and trigonometry. Much of the work undertaken in the 7th to 11th centuries AD is recognisable in the mathematics that we learn today.

Algebra

The word *Algebra* is said to have come from the word *al-jabr* which was used by Arabian mathematicians to mean 'adding equal quantities to both sides of an equation to get rid of any negative quantities', or subtracting equal quantities from both sides in order t come closer to a solution. Here are two examples.

A quantity take away 7 equals 5

$$\chi - 7 = 5$$
$$\chi - 7 + 5 = 5 + 7$$
$$\chi = 12$$

A quantity added to 4 equals 23

$$\chi + 4 = 23$$
$$\chi + 4 - 4 = 23 - 4$$
$$\chi = 19$$

It was also used to describe the way you multiply both sides of an equation to get rid of fractional quantities.

Half of a quantity equals 12

$$\tfrac{1}{2}\chi = 12$$
$$\tfrac{1}{2}\chi \times 2 = 12 \times 2$$
$$\chi = 24$$

word *al-mugabala* was used to describe the way
you collect like terms together before reducing the
ms further. For example:

subtracted from eight times a quantity equals
ce that quantity.

$$8x - 9 = 2x$$
$$8x - 2x - 9 = 2x - 2x$$
$$6x - 9 = 0$$
$$6x - 9 - 9 = 0 + 9$$
$$6x = 9$$
$$\frac{6x}{6} = \frac{9}{6}$$
$$x = 1\tfrac{3}{6} \text{ or } 1\tfrac{1}{2}$$

mathematician called Musa al-Khwarizmi wrote
oks on algebra, arithmetic, astronomy and
ography. His book on algebra called *Hisab al-jabr*
al-mugabala was written in the 9th century. The last
rt of the book was devoted to solving some algebraic
oblems about numbers. Arabs would call the
known number *the thing* or *the root of a plant* and
the quantities in the equations are numbers. Many
the problems were quite difficult, for example:

A number is multiplied by itself. The result is
added to 8. On subtracting 6 times the original
number, nothing is left. *What is the number?*
(There are two possible answers.)

is possible to find the answers by trial and error, but it
uld take a long time.

e problems below are fairly straightforward. Try using
gebra to see how quickly you can do them.

Added to 3
A quantity added to three is equal to seven.
What is that quantity?

Four times
Four times a quantity added to seven is equal to
twenty-three. *What is that quantity?*

Seven times
Seven times a quantity added to five is equal to
twice that quantity added to thirty. *What is that
quantity?*

Below are some interesting algebraic problems, written
in words. These are not as straightforward as the
previous three. *Can you solve them?*

You can check to see if you are right by going through
the algebra with your answers in. Make up your own
problems and use algebra to solve them.

How old?
A daughter is exactly one-third the
age of her mother and she has a
sister who is one-sixth of her own
age. The ages of all three amount to
50 years. *How old are each of
them?*

Mother and son
A mother's and son's ages add
together to make 80 years. If you
double the son's age it is greater
than the mother's age by 10
years. *How old are the mother
and son?*

Red and green
There are two types of counters
in a bag. There are three times
as many red counters as there
are green counters. When four
red counters and four green
counters are removed from the
bag there are four times as
many red counters as there are
green counters. *How many red
counters were there in the bag in the first place?*

Differ by one
*Find two numbers in the ratio of
4 to 5, so that if you add 6 to the
larger number and 1 to the
smaller number the square
roots of the new numbers will
differ from each other by 1.*

20 more
If you multiply two numbers together
the answer is 180. If you increase the
smaller of the two numbers by one
and then multiply the two numbers
together the new answer will be 20
more than the first answer. *What are
the numbers?*

How many ways?

Mathematical problems can often be expressed in a number of different ways, which may lead to different questions being asked.

How many different squares can you see in each of these patterns as they grow bigger?

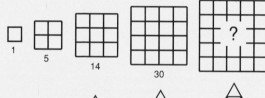

How many different triangles can you see in each of these patterns as they grow bigger?

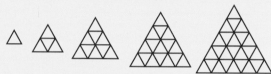

How many different rhombuses can you see in each of these patterns as they grow bigger?

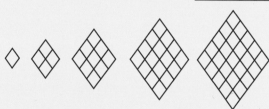

Is it possible to work out the next number in the sequence without drawing the shape?

Is it possible to work out any number in the sequence without drawing the shape?

Designs from a Chinese lattice

Other questions about counting 'how many' involve the puzzler looking for different solutions and checking that they haven't missed any possibilities out, or found 'repeat' or 'duplicate' solutions.

Try making this Chinese lattice design.

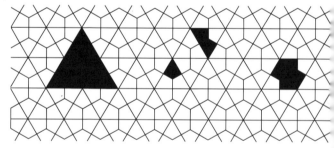

Start with a tessellation of regular hexagons.

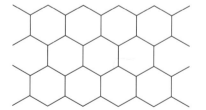

Join up the mid-point of each hexagon to the mid-point of the hexagon touching it

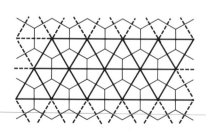

Make some copies of this Chinese lattice design. Shade in different areas on the design. *How many shapes can you find with just one line of symmetry? How about two or three lines of symmetry? Does the shape you have found have rotational symmetry?*

Can you find shapes that tessellate?

For each question, how will you know if you have found all the possible solutions or if there is a finite number of solutions?

addition to counting the ways, more mathematics ... y be involved in deciding whether one way is ... erent from another way you have found. It is not ... essarily clear as you search for your solutions.

...the following two problems you may well create ... olicas' (identical patterns) when you are searching for ... different number of ways possible in each idea. In ... se cases you will need to decide on a method for ... ecking for repeats.

...olygons into triangles

... regular polygons. By drawing lines from corner to ... ner find out how many ways you can cut the polygon ... into triangles. (You are not allowed to draw the lines ... oss other lines in this problem.)

...nes can be ... wn from corner ... corner so there ... 0 ways to cut ... shape into ... erent triangles.

1 line can be drawn from corner to corner. So there is 1 way to cut this shape into triangles.

2 lines can be drawn from corner to corner and there is one way to cut this shape into triangles.

... can use 3 lines drawn from corner to corner in the ... xagon.

...ere are 3 ways to cut the hexagon into triangles.

...olouring corners of polygons

...agine you are going to colour the corners of each of ... regular polygons using two colours. How many ways ... you colour the corners of the polygons so that each ... angement of colours is different?

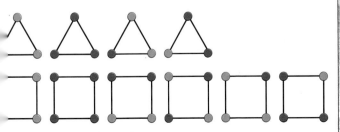

Spy lights

A spy stationed on an island worked out a way of sending messages to her accomplice on the mainland during the darkness of night. She fixed six hooks to her attic window and from these she could hang three lamps.

The battery powered lamps could have inter-changeable clear (white), red or green lenses put in them. She had enough of each lens to hang all three lamps in one colour.

By using the red, green or clear lenses in the lamps and hanging either 1, 2 or 3 lamps in different positions on the hooks, how many different signals could be sent?

Note that from a distance two white lamps placed on hooks 2 and 4 would look the same as two white lamps placed on hooks 3 and 5.

Will the spy encounter any other problems with her system?

String and knots

Cats cradles

String games are played all over the world, from the Inuits in the Arctic north to Aborigines in the hot lands of Australia. Different cultures use different materials, such as strips of sealskin, vegetable fibres and plaited human hair. The shapes made with string have often been given names, and as each pattern unfolds a story might be told.

In the United States and Great Britain this sort of string game is called 'cats cradles'. Two children can play changing the pattern of string as they pass it from one to the other.

This cats cradles puzzle actually comes from Australia. It illustrates a person climbing a tree.

Start with a loop made from two metres of smooth string. Nylon cord works well.

1. The starting position: hang the loop on your thumbs and pick up the loop with your little fingers, so that the string goes across the palms of your hands.

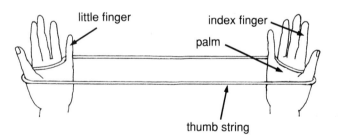

little finger   index finger
              palm

thumb string

2. With each index finger pick up the opposite string across your palms from below.

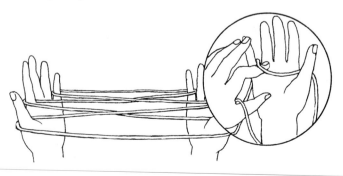

3. Take the little fingers across the top of all the strings, pick up the thumb string and pull it back. You will now have two loops on each little finger.

4. You now need to take the lower loop up and over the upper loop on each little finger. You can use your teeth to do this or the thumb and index finger of the opposite hand. Take these lower loops off the little fingers and let them lie on the far side of the index finger loops.

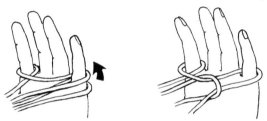

5. Bend your index fingers down to hold the bit of string across each palm.

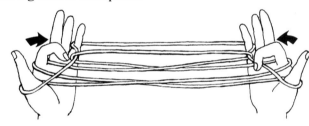

6. Hold your index fingers down tightly as you put your foot into the loop held by your little fingers. Let the string fall from your little fingers.

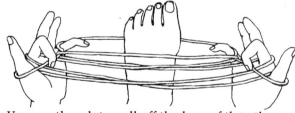

7. Use one thumb to pull off the loop of the other thumb and gently release all the fingers except the loops held under the index fingers.

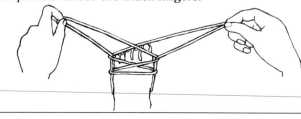

As you gently pull you will see the figure of a person climbing a tree: the diamond shape is the body and the lower triangle is the legs around the trunk (your leg). Pulling each hand alternately will make the figure climb the tree, but it gets smaller as it reaches the top.

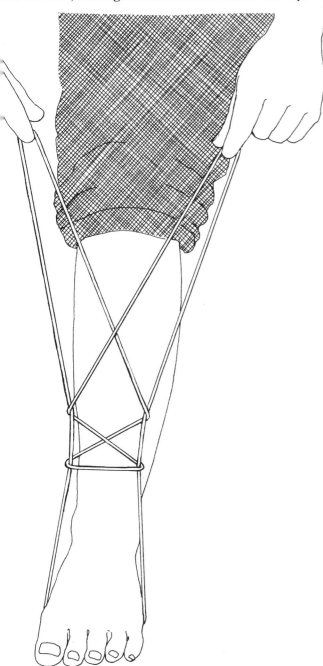

Making string shapes can be difficult so do try doing it a few times and look carefully at the diagrams. After you have perfected your string climber make up a story to go along with the making of it. The two little fingers could be birds stealing washing from the line when they loop the thumb string.

Knots and unknots

The study of knots is part of the branch of mathematics called topology (see page 46). Knots to topologists, like many other things, are slightly different to what we might think of as knots. First of all when studying knots we need to start with the unknot. The unknot is an unknotted loop of string.

This is an unknot

If you cross the unknotted loop of string it is still an unknot. *Can you see why?*

If you cross the unknot lots of times it is still an unknot. *Can you see why?*

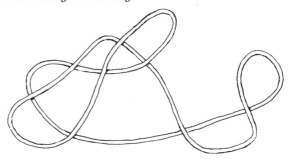

This loop of string only has three crossings – but it is a knotted loop. *Can you see why?*

Below is a knot with fourteen crossings. If you change two of the crossings it becomes an unknot. You change them by altering which part of the loop lies on top at the crossings. *Which two crossings do you need to change?*

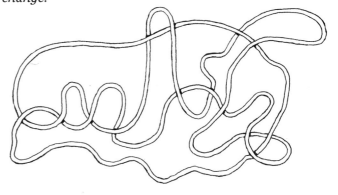

The mathematical mansion

Exit

Why do they work?

'I need half an hour to get through this marking,' thought the teacher to himself. 'I know, I shall set them an addition problem to keep them quiet.'

'I want you to sum all the numbers 1 to 1000,' said the teacher to the class.

In less than a minute the hand of Carl Gauss shot up. 'I've got the answer!' he cried. And he had, without using his slate. Carl Gauss went on to become a very distinguished mathematician. His method for solving this problem was quite straightforward.

How did Carl do it?
Well, he worked out that 1 + 999 = 1000, 2 + 998 = 1000, 3 + 997 = 1000 ... and so on.

Try summing all the numbers 1 to 10. *Do you notice anything?* Try summing 1 to 50, 1 to 100. *What is the sum of all the numbers 1 to 1000?*

Given any number series where the difference between two numbers next to each other is always the same, how could you add up all the numbers from the first to the last term?

Fast add
Ask a friend to give you a 4-digit number and write it down. **2410**

Write your own 4-digit number under it. **7589**

Ask your friend for another 4-digit number and write it down. **6823**

Again write your own 4-digit number. **3176**

Ask your friend for a final 4-digit number. **5522**
_____
25520

Offer your friend a calculator and challenge her to add the numbers before you can do it in your head. Here's how to beat her. Write 2 followed by the last 4-digit number written after subtracting 2 from it. (If the last digit was 0 it is a little more difficult.)

Can you see how it works? Try adding together single digits in the same column in the first two rows. *Why do you add and subtract 2?*

THE ANSWER IS...

```
0 + 1000 = 1000
1 +  999 = 1000
2 +  998 = 1000
3 +  997 = 1000
        ⋮
```

1 to 31
What day of the month were you born on? Look at the cards below. Select the cards the date appears on. Now add together the numbers in the top left column and that is your birthday. Think of another number between 1 and 31 and see if it works again. Try it on a friend.

8	24
9	25
10	26
11	27
12	28
13	29
14	30
15	31

A

16	24
17	25
18	26
19	27
20	28
21	29
22	30
23	31

B

2	18
3	19
6	22
7	23
10	26
11	27
14	30
15	31

C

4	20
5	21
6	22
7	23
12	28
13	29
14	30
15	31

D

1	17
3	19
5	21
7	23
9	25
11	27
13	29
15	31

E

A clue to figuring out how this works is that it involves changing numbers into base 2.

001 trick

PUT ANY 3-DIGIT NUMBER INTO YOUR CALCULATOR.

`921`

REPEAT THE NUMBER TO MAKE IT 6-DIGITS LONG.

`921921`

DIVIDE THIS NUMBER BY 13...

`70917`

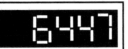

... NOW DIVIDE THIS NUMBER BY 11...

`6447`

... FINALLY DIVIDE THIS NUMBER BY 7. WHAT DO YOU GET?

IT'S THE NUMBER I STARTED WITH! DOES IT WORK FOR ANY 3-DIGIT NUMBER?

TRY IT!

ow does it work?

e 6-digit number you get when you repeat the 3-digit
mber is the same total you would get if you
ltiplied the 3-digit number by 1001.

$$
\begin{array}{r}
921 \\
\times\ 1001 \\
\hline
921000 \\
921 \\
\hline
921921
\end{array}
$$

01 has only 3 prime factors, that is prime numbers
t it can be divided by without leaving a remainder.
ey are 13, 11 and 7.

multiplying $7 \times 11 \times 13$. *What do you get?*

multiplying $921 \times 7 \times 11 \times 13$. *What do you get?*

en you divide your 6-digit number by 13, 11 and 7
u are just doing the reverse process.

Multiply the Russian way

In the last century, a method of multiplication
which involved only doubling and halving was
very popular in Russia. This is how it worked:

Take two numbers ... say, 26×48.

Put the largest number in the left-hand column.
Halve the first number and double the second.
Carry on repeating this until the first number
gets to 1.

If in the halving you get a fraction go to the next
whole number below it.

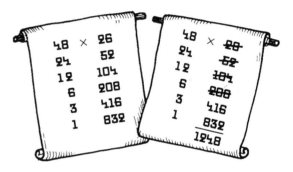

Cross out all the numbers in the right-hand
column that are opposite an even number in the
left-hand column. To get the answer add the
remaining numbers in the right-hand column.

*Can you do these multiplications
the Russian way?*

Can you multiply a 3-digit number this way?

Number shapes

Every whole number can be made with:
1 triangle number or
2 triangle numbers added together or
3 triangle numbers added together.

Some whole numbers can be made in more than one of these ways. After three, at least one branch must have more than one apple. The triangular orchard above shows how this works. How would the orchard grow for the next ten whole numbers?

WE COULD PUT ALL THE CRYSTALS INTO A SQUARE BASED PYRAMID

WE COULD PUT THEM INTO A TRIANGULAR BASED PYRAMID

Is it possible to make these pyramids with a square number of crystals?

Cube statues

These statues are made by sticking cubes together. How many for the size 3 cube? How many for the size 10 cube? If the cubes were completely hollow and were only made made up of the smaller cubes on the outside layer, how many cubes would be needed for each size cube?

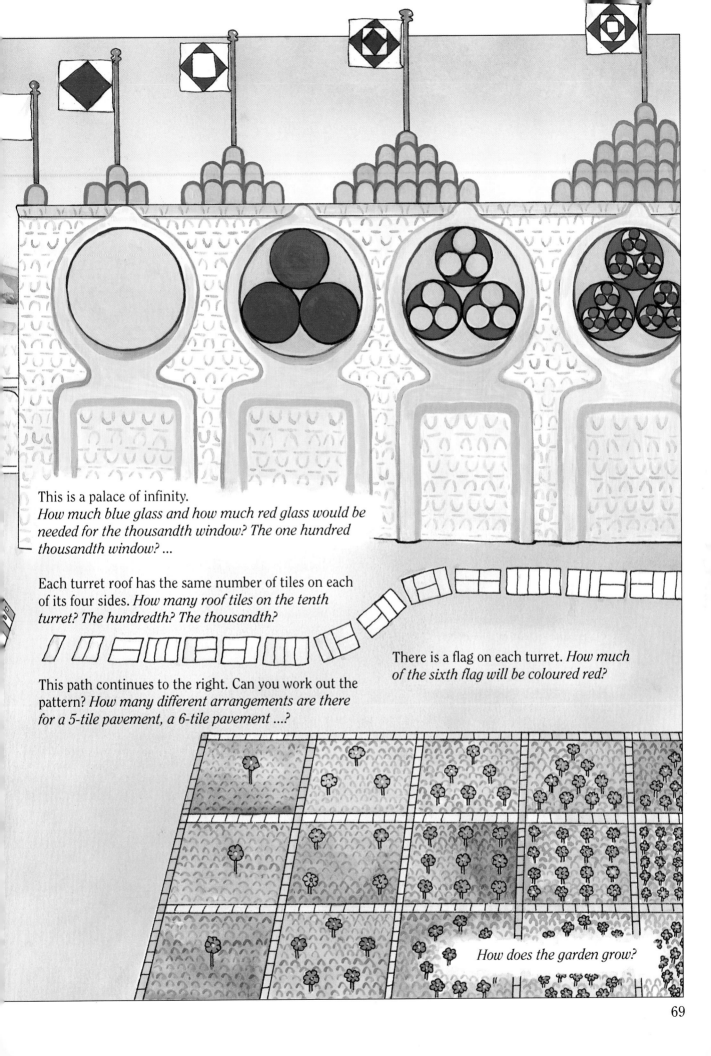

This is a palace of infinity.
How much blue glass and how much red glass would be needed for the thousandth window? The one hundred thousandth window? ...

Each turret roof has the same number of tiles on each of its four sides. *How many roof tiles on the tenth turret? The hundredth? The thousandth?*

This path continues to the right. Can you work out the pattern? *How many different arrangements are there for a 5-tile pavement, a 6-tile pavement ...?*

There is a flag on each turret. *How much of the sixth flag will be coloured red?*

How does the garden grow?

Celtic knots

The Celts first came to Britain in about 500 BC. They were a pagan people who worshipped several gods. One of the rules they had was that their gods could not be represented realistically. And so the Celts developed an elaborate art form of patterns which they used to glorify their gods and themselves.

A Celtic cross

The Celts were converted to Christianity in the seventh century AD. Their art was carried on to glorify Christ. Opposite is a stone Celtic cross. Although time has taken its toll, you can still see the interweaving pattern.

Below is a method of constructing a simple Celtic knot. *Can you draw it?* The thin construction lines should be done in pencil and rubbed away when you start to 'weave'.

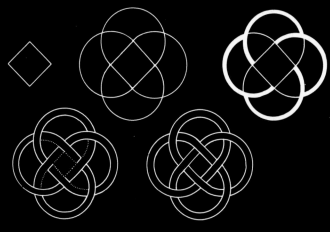

Below is another Celtic knot. *Can you construct it?*

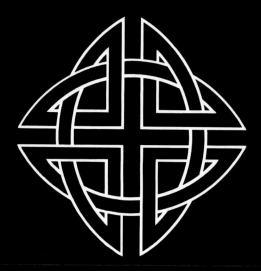

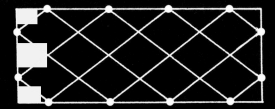

tage 1: Use a diamond grid and mark out points.

tage 2: Join the points up in light pencil. Join round the utside with arches.

tage 3: Draw a band around all the construction lines, trying keep the widths equal. Imagine the lines are a route and you re drawing the path around them.

tage 4: Rub out the construction lines and begin to weave, arting at a corner and interlacing under and over...

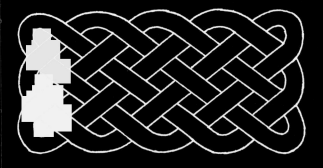

Constructing a Celtic knotwork panel

This type of knotwork interlacing is peculiar to the Picts, the people from ancient northern Britain. They discovered that certain proportions of a rectangle made up of diamonds made it possible to produce a continuous interweaving line. It was believed that such a pattern represented Eternity – everlasting life. In many cases the rules are these:

1. The number of points in the two adjoining sides have no common factor (for example, five and four, four and three).
2. The corner points mark half spaces.

In this example the top and bottom lines have four points and the two sides have two points. It is one of a few exceptions to the rule, but a fairly simple pattern to start with.

Investigate drawing your own interlacing patterns in this way.

The mathematical Picts worked very exactly, believing God would detect their errors. The inset on page 70 shows a detail from the first page of St John's Gospel from the famous Lindisfarne Gospels made in about AD 698 in the remote Northumbrian monastery on Lindisfarne. This beautiful book can be seen in the British Museum, London.

Other examples are found in the Books of Durrow, Kells and Armargh. In a detail of the Book of Armargh there are no less than 158 interlacements of a ribbon in a quarter of a square inch.

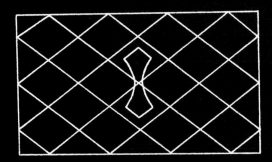

Now try some other patterns, for example four by three. Try starting with a shape in the middle which you weave around. The diamond in the grid used by the Celtic Picts was not a square but a lozenge, which is a parallelogram of four equal sides with two obtuse angles and two acute angles. You might like to try making more authentic patterns using the Pict rules. Why not use some of your designs to make an interesting greetings card?

Colourful puzzles

In 1976 Kenneth Appel and Wolfgang Haken proved that you need a maximum of four colours on a map so that the colour of any two regions next to each other are different.

Some maps can be coloured by using less than four colours. Try the following...

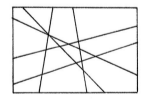

Take a sheet of paper and draw straight lines from one side of the paper to the opposite side. *What is the minimum number of colours you need to colour a map such as this?*

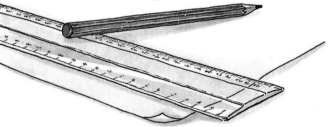

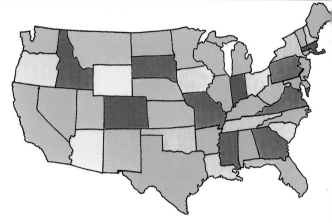

Only 4 colours are needed to colour in this map of the USA so that no two states next to each other are the same colour. *Is it possible to use fewer colours?*

Colourful solids
If a map is drawn on a sphere, what is the minimum number of colours needed for all situations?

Imagine a map drawn on a Möbius strip. Will four colours be enough to make sure that regions next to each other do not have the same colour?

Colouring edges
Imagine that you have drawn a network ...

and that you want to colour the edges on the network so that each touching edge is a different colour to the next.

What is the smallest number of colours you can use for this network so that you keep to the rule?

Draw different networks and see how many colours you need for each one. *Can you predict how many colours you will need for different types of networks.*

If you were to colour the edges of a cube so that each touching edge is a different colour, what is the minimum number of colours you need?

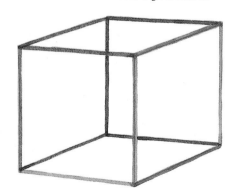

Colourful board

Draw a 5 x 5 board and take 25 counters - five counters each of five different colours. Take the first colour, say green, and place all the counters so that there are no two green counters in a horizontal, vertical or diagonal line with each other.

Fill the whole board with the 25 counters in this way so that there are never two counters of the same colour in a line with each other.

When you have done the 5 x 5 board with 25 counters, try other boards of different sizes. *Can it be done on any even board? Can it be done on any odd board?*

Making up colourful problems

Below are the nets for four cubes. Copy them, cut them out and colour them as shown. Then make them into cubes.

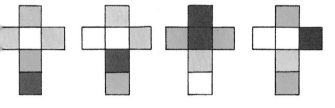

Now arrange the four cubes into a tower so that on each side of the tower all four colours are shown. Invent some similar problems.

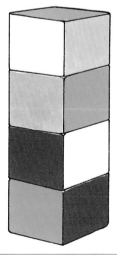

Colour cube

Paint 27 small cubes nine different colours (three cubes painted in each colour). Build a 3 x 3 x 3 cube so that there is only one of each colour showing on each side of the cube.

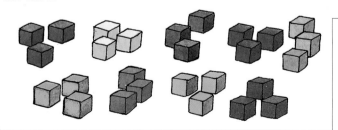

Colourful doors

Every door in a street has a number painted on it. All the odd numbers are painted blue and all the even numbers are painted yellow. *If you add a blue number to a yellow number what colour do you get?*

Cryptarithms

The word cryptarithm was coined in 1931 in a Belgian mathematical magazine. The puzzle opposite accompanied an article which said that ... 'in cryptology numbers are usually substituted for letters. In a cryptarithm it is the other way round ...' *Can you crack the code?*

$$
\begin{array}{r}
ABC \\
\times\ DE \\
\hline
FEC \\
DEC \\
\hline
HGBC
\end{array}
$$

Cracking cryptarithms

Though cryptarithms were not given a name until 1931, they have been around for a long time. It is possible to solve them without doing much arithmetic. Cryptarithms have certain conventions, that is rules which are accepted by most people who make them up or solve them.

Each letter stands for a different digit between 0 and 9. Here is an example; what can we deduce?

$$
\begin{array}{r}
BAG \\
\times\ GAB \\
\hline
A\bullet\bullet \\
\bullet\bullet B \\
\bullet B\bullet \\
\hline
\bullet G\bullet\bullet\bullet
\end{array}
$$

None of the digits can be 0 or 1 because digits have changed place in all three products.

None of the digits can be over 4 or some of the products would be more than 3 digits. So the three digits possible are 2, 3 and 4.

B cannot be a number greater than 3. If B were 4 then the product of BAG × B would consist of more than 3 digits.

Therefore, B is either 2 or 3.

G × A = B, so neither G nor A can be 2.

Therefore, B is 2.

Can you deduce any more? Can you complete the multiplication?

Sometimes you need to use a combination of deduction and trial and error to solve the cryptarithm.

Can you put two numbers made from one each of the ten digits (1234567890) to replace the spots to make a multiplication sum? Zero is not to be at the start or end of either number.

$$
\begin{array}{r}
\bullet\bullet\bullet\bullet\bullet\bullet\bullet\bullet\bullet\bullet \\
\times\ 2 \\
\hline
\bullet\bullet\bullet\bullet\bullet\bullet\bullet\bullet\bullet\bullet
\end{array}
$$

$$
\begin{array}{r}
SEND \\
+\ MORE \\
\hline
MONEY
\end{array}
\qquad
\begin{array}{r}
TEN \\
TEN \\
+\ FORTY \\
\hline
SIXTY
\end{array}
$$

There is no zero in the following two cryptarithms.

$$
\begin{array}{r}
WRONG \\
+\ WRONG \\
\hline
RIGHT
\end{array}
\qquad
\begin{array}{r}
SEAM \\
\times\ T \\
\hline
MEATS
\end{array}
$$

E is zero, 1 and 6 are not used in this cryptarithm. The letters stand for different digits. The dots stand for a digit that only shows up in the product.

$$
\begin{array}{r}
GREEN \\
\times\ RED \\
\hline
\bullet\bullet ORANGE
\end{array}
$$

ryptarithmetic game

is is a game for two players, using the letters of
e alphabet A to J and the numbers one to ten. You
l need pencils and paper.

ch player takes it in turn to devise the code to be
ed. Player One devises a code using the first 10
ters of the alphabet and keeps it hidden from
yer Two. For example:

2	3	4	5	6	7	8	9	0
C	G	J	H	E	I	A	D	B

yer Two makes up sums using the letters:

+ H

d Player One gives the answer (in code):

+ H = A

yer Two continues to make up sums using letters
til the code is cracked.

en the players swop roles.

*at strategies should you use to find out as
ickly as possible what each letter stands for?*

Arranging numbers

*Can you rearrange the numbers in this wheel so that
three numbers in a line always add up to 30?*

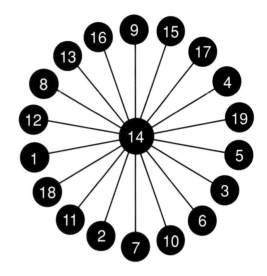

*Can you rearrange the numbers in the squares so
that all the sums are correct?*

$$1 - 2 = 3$$
$$\times$$
$$4 \div 5 = 6$$
$$=$$
$$7 + 8 = 9$$

*Can you rearrange the numbers so that the three
sides each add up to 20?*

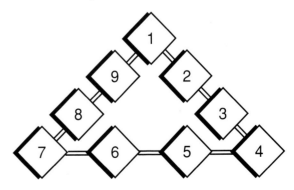

Chinese puzzle

The Chinese puzzle called the tangram is made from seven pieces cut from a single square. The five triangles, square and parallelogram can be used to make many different shapes resembling people, animals, objects and shapes.

Little is known of the origin of the tangram. It is probably very old, but the first mention of it in recorded history was in Chinese books printed about 1800. In his library Lewis Carroll had a book called *The Fashionable Chinese Puzzle*, which contained 323 tangram shapes. Though there is no date of publication, a note in the book states that the tangram was a popular pastime with Napolean whilst he was in exile. So we can assume that tangram puzzling was going on in Europe as early as 1820.

The American inventor of puzzles, Sam Loyd, claimed that the tangram was named after the legendary 'Great Tan of China', who was the first to cut the square into these seven pieces some four thousand years ago. Though a romantic thought, this is an unlikely origin of the name. The more likely story is that an American visiting China, having discovered the intriguing puzzle, used the Cantonese word for Chinese, *t'ang*, and the common European ending 'gram' to make up the word tangram.

Making numbers
Make a set of tangram pieces. The numbers one to eight are shown below. *Can you make them using all seven pieces of the tangram for each number?*

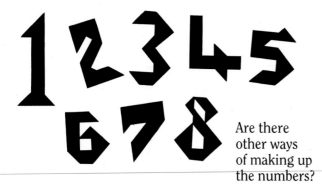

Are there other ways of making up the numbers?

Squares with holes
Obviously you can make a square using all seven tangram pieces. You can make a slightly larger square with holes using the seven pieces as well. *Can you make the squares shown below? How many of your own 'square with holes' can you make?*

Missing parallelogram?

Missing square?

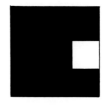

Missing triangle?

Missing 'two triangles'?

There are at least sixty different ways to make a square with two triangles missing. Here are some of the possibilities.

How many more can you find?

Squares again

A square can be made with all seven tangram pieces ...

... and one of the pieces is a square ...

Is it possible to make a square using two pieces? ... three pieces? ... four pieces? ... five pieces? ... six pieces? ...

ggram

art from the usual square tangram, tangrams have o been devised from other shapes. The rules with the gram are just the same, you must use all the pieces d no pieces should overlap. *Can you make the three ds?* Invent some shapes of your own.

Points and paths

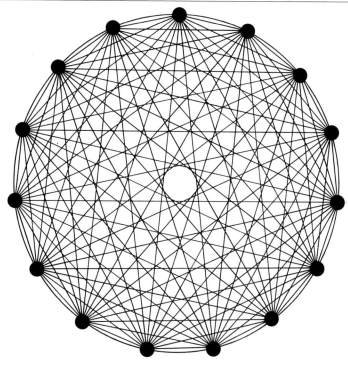

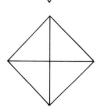

A three point mystic rose can be drawn with one continuous line.

Two continuous lines are needed to draw a four point mystic rose.

Mystic roses

A mystic rose is made by joining dots which are equally spaced around a circle. Each dot is joined to every other dot with a straight line. In 1809, a mathematician called L. Poinsot raised the question: 'What are the minimum number of continuous lines needed to draw various mystic roses?' (A continuous line is one that is drawn without lifting the pen from the paper or retracing any on the lines.)

What is the minimum number of continuous lines needed to draw the mystic roses below? (Remember, every point must be joined to every other point.)

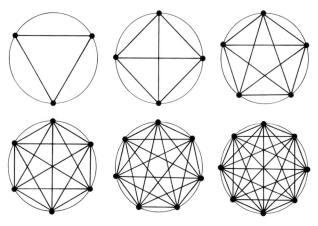

Is it possible to predict the number of continuous line for any mystic rose, no matter how many points it has?

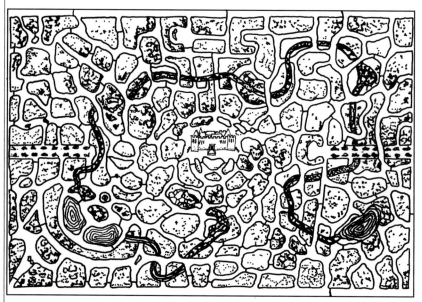

The castle in the forest

The problem of 'the castle in the forest' first appeared in *The Strand* magazine in 1903. The castle is surrounded by a forest with a winding river and green valleys. There are fences across many of the pathways to bar the way. The traveller mu reach the castle by a route which goes across a bridge and not through the river, is not barred by any fence and does not go back over any part of the way twice. The entrance is on the right-hand side. *Can you find the way to the castle?*

Mathematical trees

Mathematical trees are grown with points and branches. The smallest tree possible has 2 points and 1 branch.

This is the only tree possible

The next size tree has 3 points and 2 branches.

This is the only tree possible

This is the same tree but bent

With 4 points and 3 branches there are two possibilities.

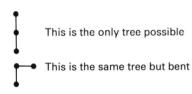

How many trees are there for 5 points and 4 branches?... 6 points and 5 branches?... 7 points and ?...

How will you make sure that your trees are definitely different?

An elephant eating buns

The drawing below is a map of an elephant house. In each room there is a bun. An elephant wants to eat all the buns without visiting any room twice. *Is it possible? If the elephant wanted to eat the least number of buns, which route should it take? What would happen if the doors were opened and closed in different ways?*

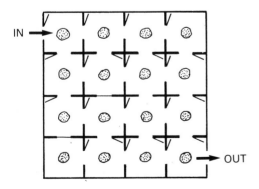

Investigate elephant houses with different numbers of rooms.

Spider and solids

Can the spider walk along all the edges of the tetrahedra in one continuous walk without retracing its path?

With the same condition can the spider walk around the edges of the polyhedra below?

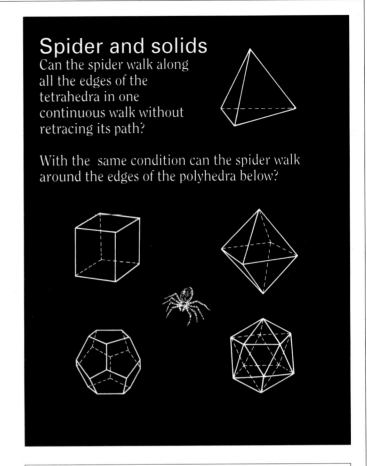

Sprouts

Sprouts is a game for two players. Dots are drawn, well apart, on a sheet of paper. The numbers of dots determines how long the game will last. Six or seven dots gives a good game. In turn, each player draws a line joining one dot to another, or a dot to itself. The player then places a dot wherever they choose along the line they have drawn. The second player does the same as the first player and so on.

Rules for sprouts
- A dot can only have a maximum of three lines leaving it. (If a line joins a dot to itself this counts as two leaving lines.)
- A line cannot cross itself or any other line.

Winning sprouts
The player who is the last one able to draw a line is the winner.

The winning line

Further ways

Arranging cans

In mathematics arranging the same items in different ways is called permutations. Take three cans of paint. *How many different ways can they be arranged?*

If there was only one can there would be only one arrangement.

With two cans ...

With three cans ...

How many ways for four cans? Five cans?

Number of ways of arranging three cans =
$1 \times 2 \times 3 = 3!$

The sum above is a factorial. 3! means multiply together successive terms from one to the number which is followed by the exclamation mark. *Can the number of arrangements of 4 and 5 cans also be calculated like this?*

The Mathematician's Tale

One April night, 'twas windy and wet,
In the Tabard Inn ten pilgrims met.
Said our host, "We need a tale,
From the Mathematician, while we sup our ale,
Be quick, tell us a puzzle of mirth and fun."
"By St Nicholas," came the reply, "it shall be done.

And so with courteous manner and good cheer,
The Mathematician's tale began, as you shall hear.

"Once, long ago, ten knights did meet,
To sing and talk, to drink and eat,
But, alas it was, they came to disagree,
Of who sat where, next to thou or thee.
One knight drew his sword, and then another,
And each brother knight then slew each other.
The room was soon dark, coloured red,
As ten foolish knights lay dying or dead.
That night upon them a curse was lain,
That only arithmetic could explain.

Eating out

The café offers a choice of five starters, eight main courses and four puddings. You dine there each day on a three course meal. Every day you have a different meal. *If the café opened on 1 March, on what date would you have had all the possible combinations of meals?*

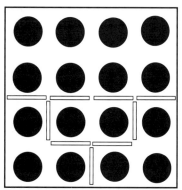

Alphabet

How many different arrangements of all the letters of the alphabet can be made? You may use each letter only once in each arrangement.

AB, AC, AD, AE, ...

Arranging fences

In a certain city square there stood 16 statues within a low wall arranged as in the grid below. Every year the mayor of the city places 9 movable fences so as to divide the statues into different size groups. In the arrangement below the statues are divided into groups of 8, 3, 3 and 2. This year the mayor wants to arrange the statues into groups of 6, 6 and 4. *Can he do it by moving only 2 fences? 3 fences? 4 fences? 5 fences? 6 fences? 7 fences?*

this point the mathematician drew breath,
e all called out, "Tell us of their after-death!"

he ghosts were to meet each year to dine,
d sit in different positions each time,
l the variations must they make,
less they could predict the number it take.
r only when the answer could be found,
uld the ten knights be heavenly bound."

e actuary declared, "To my mind then,
e knights could move from one to ten."
o," said our host, "with ten people at table,
least a hundred times are able."
ar more, I think," said the good nun,
is an even greater sum!"

w this puzzle I put to you,
w many permutations are possible to do?

Puzzle mazes

It should not be too difficult to thread a maze which is drawn on paper. The one below is called 'The Philadelphia Maze', which was invented by the great puzzler Henry Dudeney. *Can you find a route from A to B?*

Once you have found a route try this puzzle: *If you are not allowed to go down the same passage twice, how many routes are there altogether from A to B?* You may regard the shaded areas as hallways, which can be travelled along as many times as you like.

nry Dudeney devoted a whole chapter to 'Mazes and how to thread them' in his book *Amusements in* *thematics*. Many of the other puzzles which he collected were also 'maze like' in their concept. Here are election of his maze-like puzzles.

oving engines

e aim of this puzzle is to move all the engines around
tracks so that they finally end up in numerical order
und the circle. The central crossing point is a
ntable allowing engines to leave on whichever track
·y want to, but it is to be left empty at the end. Only
) engines can fit on each section of the circular track.
e engines can go forwards or backwards. One of the
gines cannot move. *Which engine stays still? How do*
· *others move to solve the problem?*

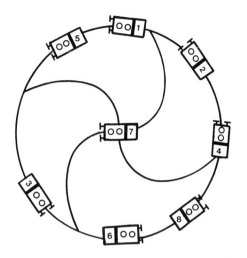

The white bishop

The white bishop has decided to visit each of his parishes. These are represented by the white squares on the
chessboard. He may pass through his parishes more
than once, but he is not allowed to travel the same path
again. Each move is like the white bishop's in the game
of chess. This means he can go diagonally along any
number of the white squares, in a straight line and in
any direction. *What is the smallest number of moves he*
can do to complete his task?

aths in a grid

:h path must be travelled along at least once. *What is the shortest route you can take around the grid?*
estigate with other sized grids.

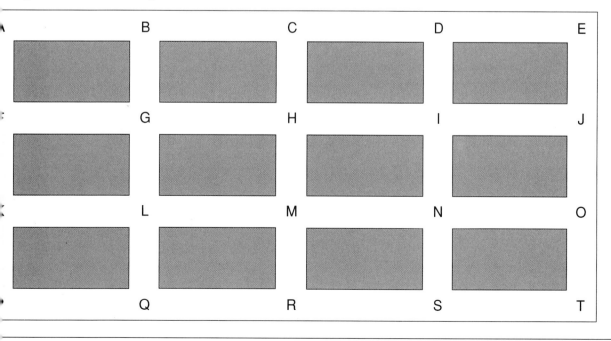

Calculate it!

In 1780 an American slave called Thomas Fuller was asked to say how long he had lived, in seconds. At the time, he was 70 years and 17 days old.

It took him just 90 seconds to work out the answer in his head. The person who had asked the question used pencil and paper and took much longer to come up with an answer. The two answers disagreed, the pencil and paper solution was less than Thomas Fuller's. Fuller pointed out that his was the correct solution, because in his mental calculation he had also included the extra days in the leap years.

Thomas Fuller was born in Africa in 1710. In 1724 he was taken prisoner and transported to Virginia in the USA as a slave. He was never taught to read or write, but he did have amazing abilities with mental arithmetic. In his head he was able to do such things as multiply two nine-digit numbers together and work out how many grains of wheat there were in a given weight.

In your head

How quickly can you work out how long you have lived in seconds? Can you work it out in your head? ... on paper? ... or using a calculator?

Today we use calculators to speed up calculations. They also bring difficult mathematical puzzles and problems within our reach.

Though many puzzles may have one unique answer, that does not necessarily mean there is only one way of arriving at that solution. The most important thing is to develop your own ways of solving puzzles and problems. The variety of methods used to solve a puzzle can be as interesting as the puzzle itself.

Divided

I have divided a one-digit number by another one-digit number and the answer on my calculator is 0.4 What were my two numbers?

I have divided another one-digit number by a one-digit number and the answer is 0.2222222 What were my two numbers?

Is there a way to find the answer quickly? Try inventi similar problems for friends to solve. If one-digit problems are easy, go on to larger numbers.

few keys

magine that you can only use the following keys on ur calculator:

at numbers between 1 and 50 can you make with m? Did you make these numbers by using the allest number of key presses possible?

u can make 18 by pressing twelve keys:

t

o makes 18 and you only press six keys.

u can make similar problems for yourself by anging the numbers and the signs that you are owed to use.

ultiplication chains

art with a number   372
ltiply the digits together
7 x 2 = 42
ep multiplying   4 x 2 = 8
til you are left with only one digit.
372 took two steps to finish.

ich number below 500 takes the greatest number of ps to finish?

axing island

a remote island of Egret, the ruling elders have a ecial system of taxation. Islanders are taxed such that ey pay the same percentage in taxes as they earn in ousands. So for example someone who earns 4 000 zricks would pay 4% of these earnings to the island, d someone who earns 75 000 Nazricks would pay % of these earnings to the island.

at amount of money would you like to earn so that u are left with the most money after you have paid ur taxes?

Sequences

You can make up rules to generate sequences of numbers. Sometimes the sequences end up in a particular place. The following two problems are about repeating rules. Try to see what is happening and predict what will happen for any start numbers combined with any rule.

Work with one number to start with — 7

Divide your number by 3 and then add 1 — 3.3333333

Divide your new number by 3 and then add 1 to get the next number — 2.1111111

Keep repeating the rule until you notice something. Investigate with different starting numbers and the same rule. Try different rules.

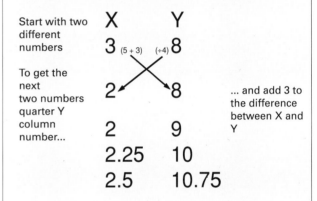

Start with two different numbers

To get the next two numbers quarter Y column number...

... and add 3 to the difference between X and Y

X	Y
3 (5 + 3)	(÷4) 8
2	8
2	9
2.25	10
2.5	10.75

Predict what will happen with different starting numbers in each of the columns. Predict what will happen with different rules for each of the columns.

85

Three in a row

Tic-tac-toe has been played by many different peoples for thousands of years. Tic-tac-toe boards have been found carved on the walls of ancient Egyptian temples. The game was also played in China in 500 BC. The Romans played it as well. You can find tic-tac-toe boards in English cathedrals, which were carved into the seats by monks in the fourteenth century.

Tic-tac-toe is the oldest surviving game which is played by two opponents where no element of luck is used to determine the outcome. Other games of this sort include noughts and crosses, which is a development of tic-tac-toe, nim, draughts and its variations. It is possible to work out a strategy for all these games so that you never lose.

Playing Tic-tac-toe
Below is a drawing of a tic-tac-toe board. The rules of the game are as follows: each player has a set of three counters, one set is white, the other is black. The players start by placing their counters alternately on vacant points of the board. When all the counters have been placed on the board play begins ... Each player, in turn, then moves one of their counters along a straight line to a neighbouring vacant point. The winner is the first player to get a line of three with their counters. *Which is the best point to put your counter on to start with? Does the player who goes first have an advantage over the other player? Is there always a winner?*

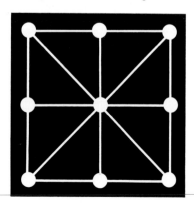

First or second
In many games between two players the one who has the first move is considered to have an advantage. *Is this true in the following games?*

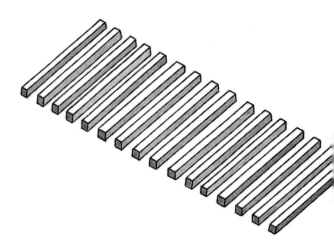

16 sticks are laid out in a line. A player may take 1 or sticks away from the pile each turn. The player who takes the last stick is the winner. *Is it possible for the first or the second player to win all the time? Why?*

In this version of the game only 9 sticks are laid out. *Again, does it matter who goes first?*

Rule change
What happens if the rule is changed so that the playe who takes the last stick is the loser?

What number of sticks would the player who goes firs choose if they wanted to win?

What number of sticks would the player who goes second choose to have if they wanted to win?

Nim

The game of nim probably came from China. It is a game for two players using three piles of sticks. This time each player takes 1 or 2 sticks away from any one pile in turn. *Is this game fairer for the first or the second player?*

Take away more

The rules are changed so that instead of just allowing each player to take only 1 or 2 sticks, they are allowed to take 3, 4 or 5 sticks away. *Does this make a difference? What happens if there are more piles of sticks at the beginning of the game?*

3-D noughts and crosses

This game is a more difficult variation of 2-D noughts and crosses. To play it you will need to copy out the diagram below.

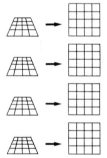

As in the 2-D version of noughts and crosses each player places their mark (the nought or the cross) in any vacant square on the grid. This time, you need to get a row of 4 noughts, or 4 crosses to win the game. The winning lines are more complicated as well, because they can be made both with straight and diagonal lines through the four boards, as well as the straight lines on any of the boards.

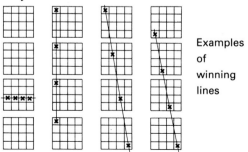

Examples of winning lines

Counters

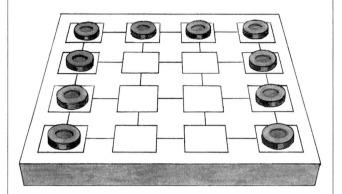

Above is a puzzle with counters. Counters can only move by making a vertical or horizontal jump over another counter. (Diagonal jumps are not allowed!) A 'jumped-over' counter is removed from the board. The idea of the puzzle is to take all but one counter off the board. In order to start you may move one counter into any unoccupied square.

Reversing

1. Using draught-like moves (either sliding into a vacant square or jumping over one counter into a vacant space) reverse the order of the counters to 5, 4, 3, 2, 1. *What is the smallest number of moves you need to do this?*

2. Add a seventh square and a sixth counter. *What is the smallest number of moves needed to reverse the order now?*

3. *If you had a strip of a million squares and 999 999 counters what would be the minimum number of moves needed to reverse the order?*

Island routes

Problems which involve taking the right route, drawing the right path or making the right connections are both maze-like and mathematical. The maze part happens when you find a solution to your problem; the mathematics happens when you are searching for the answer and checking that it is right, and again later when you investigate other situations. Each of these island routes has a solution and each problem offers many other possibilities for exploration.

Some island problems

The following problem is about connecting islands to each other with bridges.

There are three islands and it must be possible for everyone on each of the islands to visit one another. With two bridges there is only one way of connecting them.

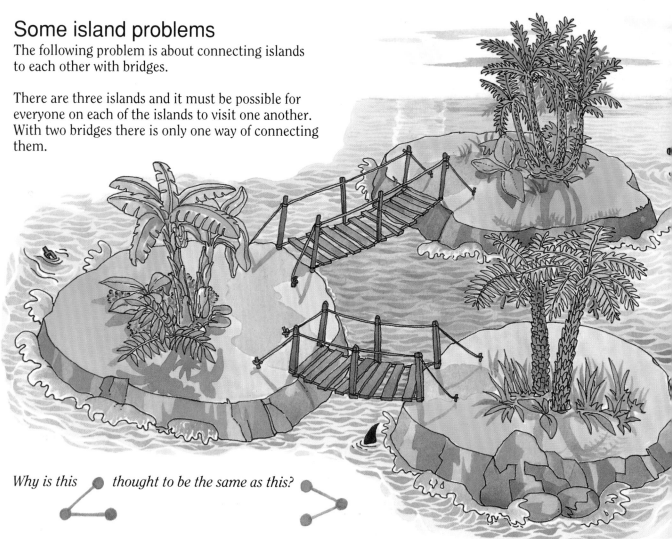

Why is this ● *thought to be the same as this?*

With four islands and three bridges how many different ways are there of connecting them so that everyone can visit all four islands?

What happens if there are five islands and four bridges? Investigate different connections for other numbers of islands.

A further island problem

With six islands is it possible to connect them so that: three islands have three bridges going from them, two islands have two bridges going from them, and one island has just one bridge going from it?

88

Delivering supplies

The map opposite shows the route a ship travelled when delivering supplies to five islands. If you tried to repeat the journey starting at island A and following the arrowed directions, you would find that it is impossible without visiting some of the islands more than once. *Which island could the ship have started from to complete the route sucessfully?* The ship can travel along each path once and once only, and only in the direction shown by the arrows. *Which other routes could the ship have taken? Which island could the ship be at now?*

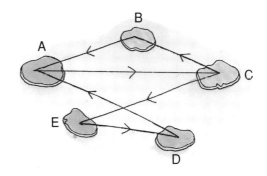

Here are some other maps for you to think about. One of them cannot be successfully followed without changing the direction of one of the arrows. *Which map? Which arrow?*

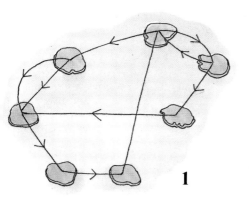

1

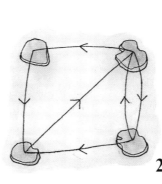

2

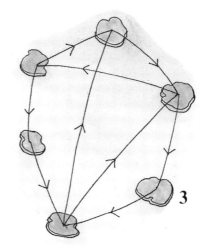

3

On board ship

The wind has dropped and the sea is calm. On board the ship the crew have trimmed the sails and scrubbed the decks. They settle down to discuss a problem put by Rowenta, the captain.

She says, 'There are 30 crew members and here are 30 pineapples and 10 coconuts. How could the fruit be arranged in a circle so that if the 30 members of the crew each took every twelfth fruit there would only be the 10 coconuts left on the deck?' *How could this problem be made much simpler?*

Try 3 members of the crew, 3 pineapples and 1 coconut and take every third fruit.

Curious squares

The magic square below was found in Khajuraho, India. Although it is not the earliest magic square, it does date back to the twelfth century.

7	12	1	14
2	13	8	11
16	3	10	5
9	6	15	4

What is a magic square?

The simplest type of magic square is an arrangement of numbers on a grid of cells that form a square. The numbers in the square should be placed so that the rows, columns and two main diagonals all sum to the same total. The numbers used in a real magic square must be the same as the number of cells in the square, e.g. a 3 x 3 square has the numbers 1 to 9 in it; a 4 x 4 square has 1 to 16; a 5 x 5 square has 1 to 25; and so on.

52	61	4	13	20	29	36	45
14	3	62	51	46	35	30	19
53	60	5	12	21	28	37	44
11	6	59	54	43	38	27	22
55	58	7	10	23	26	39	42
9	8	57	56	41	40	25	24
50	63	2	15	18	31	34	47
16	1	64	49	48	33	32	17

Franklin's square

In about 1750, Benjamin Franklin constructed the square above. The numbers 1 to 64 (8 x 8) are used to construct it. All the rows and columns add up to 260. But there are also some other curious discoveries to be made...

● Add the numbers in either half in any row. What is the total? Add the numbers in either half of any column. What is the total?
● What is the total if you add up the four corner numbers and add it to the sum of the four middle numbers?
● If you add up the bent diagonals (A to A etc., as shown in the diagram) on Franklin's square, what totals do you get?
● Add up any block of four cells. What totals do you get?

Are there any other curious properties in the square?

The first magic square

Constructing magic squares has been an amusement for many centuries. Originally they were thought to have mystical qualities. The drawing below is called the Loh-shu. It first made its appearance in China in about 2800 BC. Can you see why it is a magic square of the order 3?

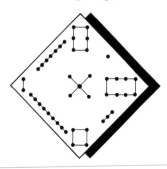

Euler's square

1	48	31	50	33	16	63	18
30	51	46	3	62	19	14	35
47	2	49	32	15	34	17	64
52	29	4	45	20	61	36	13
5	44	25	56	9	40	21	60
28	53	8	41	24	57	12	37
43	6	55	26	39	10	59	22
54	27	42	7	58	23	38	11

The curious square above was constructed by the eighteenth-century Swiss mathematician Leonhard Euler. Why is it not a magic square? Can you find any interesting properties in it? If you place a knight on the top left cell, you can land on all the numbers 1 to 64, in numerical order, by making knight's moves between them.

Magic tracing

The patterns below were drawn by tracing over magic squares in numerical order.

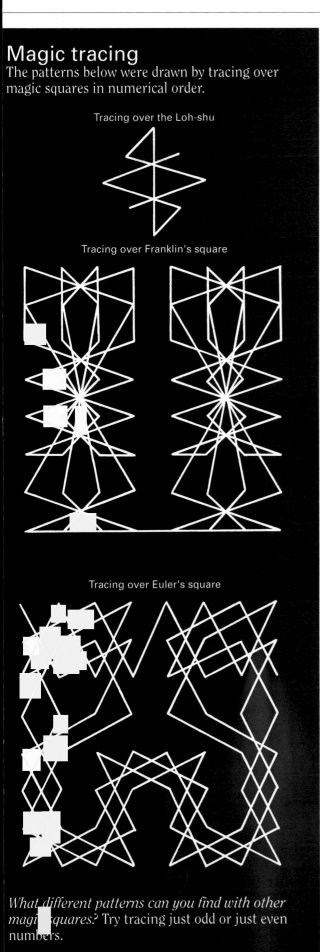

Tracing over the Loh-shu

Tracing over Franklin's square

Tracing over Euler's square

What different patterns can you find with other magic squares? Try tracing just odd or just even numbers.

Talisman square

This is a Talisman square with a constant of 1...

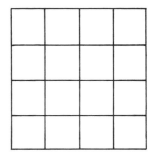

... because if you look at any one number in the square and then find the difference with each of its neighbours, this 'difference' is greater than 1.

Can you put the numbers 1 to 16 onto this grid to make a Talisman square with a constant of 2 (all the differences greater than 2)?

Is it possible to use the numbers 1 to 16 to make a square with a constant of 3?

Try Talisman squares of different sizes.

Making odd squares

The following is a method for creating a magic square of the order 3. Always start by putting the 1 in the middle cell of the top row, then place the rest of the numbers (2 to 9) by making an upward diagonal move to the right. If you come out at the top of the column return on the bottom. If the cell is occupied, put the number directly under the last number you placed. Try this method for a 5 x 5 square. Does it work for a 7 x 7 square? Will it work for any odd numbered square?

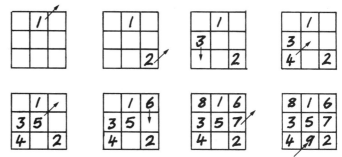

Modest indeed

When she taught the king to play chess, he was so pleased that he said she could have any reward she wished. She thought for a moment and then said: 'I am a modest creature, so I'll go for a modest reward. Just place one gold coin on the first square of the chessboard for me, then double on the next and then double that on the next, and so on, until there's a pile on every square'. *Do you think this was a modest reward?*

Number patterns

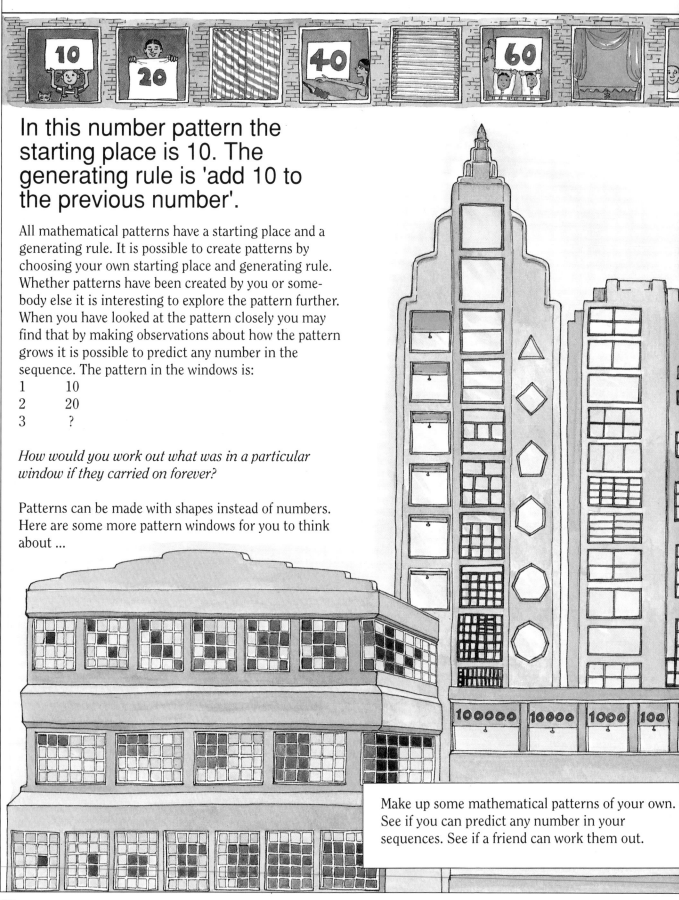

In this number pattern the starting place is 10. The generating rule is 'add 10 to the previous number'.

All mathematical patterns have a starting place and a generating rule. It is possible to create patterns by choosing your own starting place and generating rule. Whether patterns have been created by you or somebody else it is interesting to explore the pattern further. When you have looked at the pattern closely you may find that by making observations about how the pattern grows it is possible to predict any number in the sequence. The pattern in the windows is:

1   10
2   20
3   ?

How would you work out what was in a particular window if they carried on forever?

Patterns can be made with shapes instead of numbers. Here are some more pattern windows for you to think about ...

Make up some mathematical patterns of your own. See if you can predict any number in your sequences. See if a friend can work them out.

Digital roots

When we look at sets of numbers according to a rule we may also observe patterns that we didn't realise were there.

All numbers have digital roots. This is how you can find the digital root of a number:

Add the digits until a single digit number is reached.

48	4 + 8
12	1 + 2
3	

3 is the digital root of 48.

You can find the digital root of sequences of numbers and see some interesting patterns emerge.

3 times table

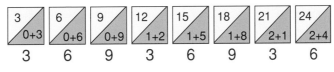

How will the pattern of digital roots of the 3 times table continue?

4 times table

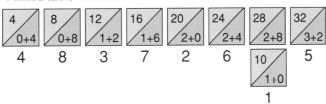

Investigate other times tables.

Triangle numbers

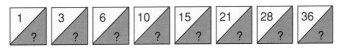

... Square ...

What happens with other types of numbers?

Exploring rules ...

Can you see how these rules were generated?

2	3	5	8	3	1	4	5	9	4	3	7	0	7	7	4
8	2	0	2	2	4	6	0	6	6	2	8	0	8	8	6

When you have discovered the rule use the same rule to see what would happen for different pairs of starting numbers.

These patterns were created in a similar way. *Can you discover the rule?*

2	3	0	3	3	1	4	0	4	4	3	2	0	2	2	4
1	4	5	2	0	2	2	4	6	3	2	5	0	5	5	3

... and building upwards

When you have created a pattern according to a rule you can use the pattern to create a new pattern. The patterns below have been built in this way.

What will happen to each triangle as it grows?

What will happen if you make more triangles?

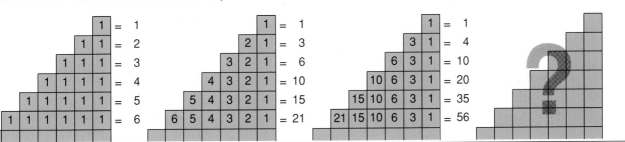

93

Miz mazes

When we think of mazes we usually think of them as puzzles to solve. We might picture many paths surrounded by tall hedges so that we can't see where we're going. The problem with these mazes is to find the middle and then the way out. But these puzzle mazes are a relatively recent invention in the history of mazes.

Before them the church mazes and miz mazes were very common. The church mazes were to be found in Europe and North Africa. The miz mazes, sometimes called mize mazes, troy towns, shepherd's races or Julian's bowers, were found in England. These miz mazes were cut into the turf and were usually made close to a church, or near an old monastery. They were often copies of the continental church mazes that pilgrims had visited. (Pilgrims are people who travel to sacred places as an act of religious faith.)

In most cases, the raised turf path was the part to follow, with the hollows on either side being the 'walls'. Though in some cases it would be the other way round and the raised turf was the walls and the hollows the pathway. Sadly, only eight turf mazes have survived into the twentieth century. Although many have been ploughed up some records of their existence remain.

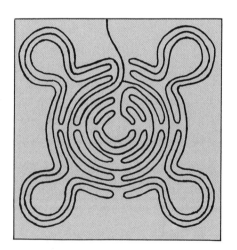

Turf maze at Sneiton, Nottinghamshire.

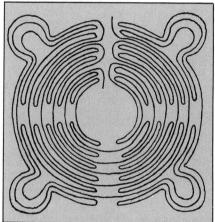

Turf maze at Saffron Waldon.

Miz maze on St Catherine's Hill, Hants.

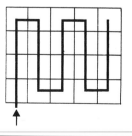

Rectangular mazes

Start at 'A' and draw a line through the centre of all the other squares once and once only. Your line must not cross at the corners. *How many miz-maze patterns can you make in this sized rectangle?* You can start at any outside square to make your maze.

Investigate miz-maze patterns using other sized rectangles.

Nine men's morris

The nine men's morris is filled up with mud;
And the quaint mazes in the wanton green
For lack of tread are indistinguishable:

A Midsummer Night's Dream, Act II, Scene ii

In Shakespeare's play, *A Midsummer Night's Dream,*
Titania talks of nine men's morris being filled up with
mud. This was a fourteenth-century game that could be
played either on a board or on a village green, with the
pattern cut out of the turf with a trowel.

Nine men's morris, which is also known as *morelles,
jeu de moulin* and *merels,* was played across Europe in
the Middle Ages. It is a game for two players and
involves placing counters in such a way so as to block
and capture the opponent.

The rules

Each player has nine counters of a different colour to
the other player's counters. The object of the game is to
remove all but two of the opponent's counters, or make
it impossible for the opponent to move any counter.

Stage 1 of the game:
Each player, in turn, places a counter at any free point
where lines meet, with the aim of getting three
counters in a row. This is known as getting a 'mill'.

Every time a mill is made a player can remove an
opponent's counter from the board. A counter already
in a mill cannot be removed unless there is no other
counter to be taken. Once off the board, a counter is
out of play for the rest of the game.

Players continue in turns until they have put down all
eighteen counters.

Stage 2:
The counters can now be moved around the board, one
place at a time, in alternate turns. A mill may be
'opened', by moving a counter along, and then re-made
in the next turn. Each time a mill is formed, or re-
formed, an opponent's counter can be taken.
A move must be made each time, even if it means
losing a counter to the opponent on the next move.

The loser is the player who is left with only two
counters, or is completely blocked by his or her
opponent.

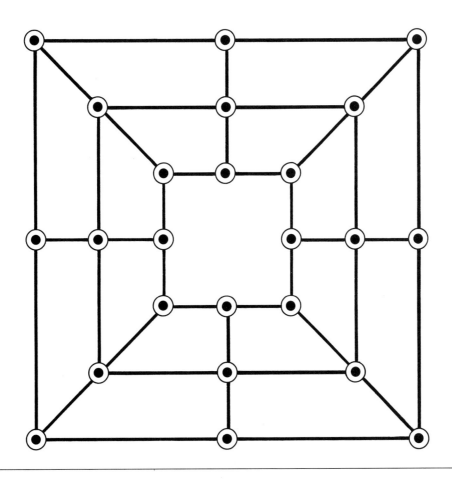

The Maya

Until the arrival of Christopher Columbus in 1492 the peoples of North and South America had not been influenced by any outside cultures. Different civilisations in the Americas came and went. These included those of the Olmec, Maya, Toltec, Mixtec and Aztec.

Of these civilisations the Maya were the most advanced in mathematics. At its peak, between AD 300 to 1000, the civilisation covered an area in South America as large as the United Kingdom.

The Maya did not have any metal tools or weapons. Nor did they have wheels. The Maya were completely dependent on human labour for their agricultural output and transportation. Yet they were able to build cities bigger than many in Europe at the same time. The Maya also developed a written language which they used to record events in their calendar. The Mayan calendar system was far more accurate than the Julian calendar used by the invaders from Western Europe in the 16th century.

Our knowledge of the Mayan world is not very full. The Spanish, who first arrived, did not try to understand the existing culture and they destroyed nearly all of the written records. Only three manuscripts survive. Most of our information comes from either Spanish accounts of previous accounts passed on by word of mouth, or from the study of Mayan hieroglyphics carved onto stone.

These hieroglyphics were very difficult to decipher, but fortunately a spoken version descended from the Mayan language survived. Using this we now know the meanings of 500 of the 800 known hieroglyphics.

As with many civilisations, written records, and especially carved ones, were made at the direction of the various priesthoods and were to do with their calendar, recording great events or when official religious events should take place during the year. Because of this we may have a distorted view of a people totally dominated by the calculation of the year.

Mayan number system

The Maya developed a written system of numbers base on 18 and 20.

In our decimal system place values go up in tens and 61 924 would be written under the following place headings:

10 000	1000	100	10	1
6	1	9	2	4

In the Mayan system these are the first five place value with the number 61 924 under the headings:

18×20^3 $= 144\,000$	18×20^2 $= 7200$	18×20 $= 360$	20	1
0	8	12	0	4

The Maya did not write their numbers with the Hindu-Arabic numerals that we use. Their system was much simpler.

● (a dot or pebble) stood for one and | (a stick) stood f five. 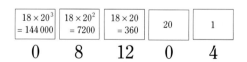 (a shell) stood for zero and was used as a plac

der when there were no numbers of that value. The
[Ma]ya wrote their numbers from bottom to top. This is
[ho]w they would have written the number 61 924:

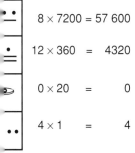

$8 \times 7200 = 57\ 600$

$12 \times 360\ \ = \ \ \ 4320$

$0 \times 20\ \ \ = \ \ \ \ \ \ \ \ 0$

$4 \times 1\ \ \ \ = \ \ \ \ \ \ \ \ 4$

*Can you translate these Mayan numbers into
our decimal system?*

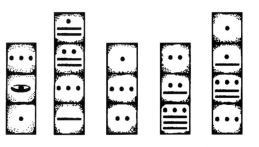

Surprising numbers

$$1^2 = 1$$
$$11^2 = 121$$
$$111^2 = 12321$$
$$1111^2 = 1234321$$
$$11111^2 = 123454321$$
$$111111^2 = 12345654321$$

$$9^3 = 729$$
$$99^3 = 970299$$
$$999^3 = 997002999$$
$$9999^3 = 999700029999$$

$$4^2 = 16$$
$$34^2 = 1156$$
$$334^2 = 111556$$
$$3334^2 = 11115556$$
$$33334^2 = 1111155556$$

$$9^2 = 81$$
$$99^2 = 9801$$
$$999^2 = 998001$$
$$9999^2 = 99980001$$
$$99999^2 = 9999800001$$

$$3 \times 37 = 111$$
$$6 \times 37 = 222$$
$$9 \times 37 = 333$$
$$12 \times 37 = 444$$
$$15 \times 37 = 555$$
$$18 \times 37 = 666$$

$$1 \div 9 = 0.11111 \ldots$$
$$2 \div 9 = 0.22222 \ldots$$
$$3 \div 9 = 0.33333 \ldots$$
$$4 \div 9 = 0.44444 \ldots$$
$$5 \div 9 = 0.55555 \ldots$$

$$1 + 2 = 3$$
$$4 + 5 + 6 = 7 + 8$$
$$9 + 10 + 11 + 12 = 13 + 14 + 15$$
$$16 + 17 + 18 + 19 + 20 = 21 + 22 + 23 + 24$$

Do all these patterns continue?

$$483 \times 12 = 5796$$
$$297 \times 18 = 5346$$
$$157 \times 28 = 4396$$

*What do you notice about these multiplications?
Can you make any more?*

```
  12345679
×         8
  98765432
×         9
 888888888
```

```
 123456789
 123456789
 987654321
 987654321
+        2
2222222222
```

Do these add up?

$$3 \times 1 = 3$$
$$3 \times 2 = 6$$
$$3 \times 3 = 9$$
$$3 \times 4 = 12 \qquad 1 + 2 = 3$$
$$3 \times 5 = 15 \qquad 1 + 5 = 6$$
$$3 \times 6 = 18 \qquad 1 + 8 = 9$$

$$3 \times \ \ 99 = 297 \qquad 2 + 9 + 7 = 18 \qquad 1 + 8 = 9$$
$$3 \times 100 = 300 \ldots$$

Have you spotted the pattern?

Liars, hats and logic

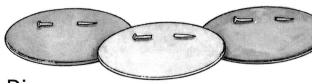

Discs

A man and a woman were sitting in a room. A third person entered the room and said, 'Here are three dis[cs], two blue and one red. I shall pin one disc on each of your backs and put the third one in my pocket witho[ut] either of you seeing its colour. You will then be able t[o] see the disc on each other's back. The first one who c[an] tell me the colour of the disc pinned to their back sh[all] receive the prize.

The man looked at the disc on the woman's back but remained silent. The woman then knew the colour of her disc and she claimed the prize. *What was the colour of her disc and how did she know?*

THIS SQUARE IS BLANK

Logical paradoxes

In the sixth century BC, Epimenides made the following statement:

'All Cretans are liars.'

Epimenides was a Cretan. *Can you see the problem with his statement?*

Which of the following two statements below is true?

THE SENTENCE BELOW IS TRUE.

THE SENTENCE ABOVE IS FALSE.

A woman, a child and a tiger.

A mother and her child were out working in the field. Suddenly a tiger appeared and took hold of the child. 'Give me back my child, ' pleaded the woman. 'I will,' replied the tiger, 'if you can correctly predict the fate of your child - either that I eat him or I give back to you unharmed.' 'You will eat him' said the woman'. *What do you think was the fate of the child?*

Five hats

Three women sat in a row, one behind the other. All three were blindfolded. 'Here are five hats,' said a fourth woman, 'two green hats and three yellow. I shall place one hat on each of your head[s] and put the other two hats into the cupboard. Yo[u] may then remove your blindfolds. But, you must remain seated and you cannot turn your head. The one who can tell me what colour hat she is wearing will receive a prize.' The fourth woman then put the hats on and put the other two into

More about hats

ow many different combinations of hats to heads
e possible with five hats and three women?

ow many different combinations of hats to heads
e possible with seven hats and three women? ...
ne hats? ... Eleven hats? ...

ed and green hats

ree men and one woman were sitting facing each
her. All were blindfolded. A fifth person announced
at she would place either a red or a green hat on
ch of them. They should then remove their
ndfolds and if they saw a red hat then they should
nd on their chair. If they could correctly state the
lour of their own hat they should stand on the
ble.

ly red hats were put on the four heads. When the
ndfolds were removed, all four stood on their
airs. After a while the woman climbed onto the
ble. *How did she work out the colour of her hat?*

he cupboard.
'he woman at the back of the row removed her
lindfold and saw the two hats in front of her, but
he remained silent. The woman in the middle
emoved her blindfold and saw one hat. She also
emained silent. The woman at the front of the
ow did not remove her blindfold, nevertheless
he correctly stated the colour of her own hat
nd claimed the prize. *Can you work out the*
olour of her hat? How did she know?

Who got what?

Six of the children who lived in a road shared the
same birthday though they were all born in different
years. Can you work out, from the following
information, the age of each child and which of the
three types of birthday gift they received?

1 Alan and the five
   year old got a paint
   box.

2 Ellen and the 6 year
   old each got a set of
   colouring pencils.

3 Both the 7 year old
   and the 8 year old
   got felt- tipped pens.

4 Betty and Fred go to
   a different school to
   the 7 year old,
   whose hobby is
   stamp collecting.

5 Betty, who will be 9
   years old on her
   next birthday, and
   the 5 year old are
   shorter than Charlie.

6 The 9 year old has
   red hair, unlike
   Charlie.

7 The 10 year old likes
   ice cream and is
   taller than Charlie.

8 Charlie got felt- tipped
   pens and one of the
   other boys got a set of
   colouring pencils.

9 Alan is not as tall as Charlie.

To help solve the 'Who got what?' problem it may be
useful to draw a grid like this.

NAME	5	6	7	8	9	10	GIFT
A							
B							
C							
D							
E							
F							

Puzzle your way in

Can you puzzle your way to the centre and choose the right flower?

1. The queen's gardeners had planted a single rose in these two triangular flowerbeds. She had ordered that the roses should be at the centre point between top and bottom. Alas, they planted one incorrectly. *Which colour rose is correctly positioned?*

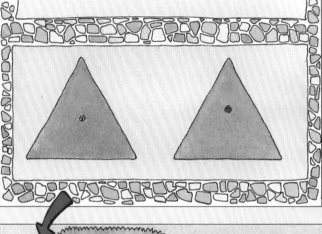

7. One of the girls had spilt paint all over the lawn.
'It's too much,' said the queen of clubs, 'which one of you did it?'
Ruby said, 'Scarlet just poured the paint over the grass. I didn't spill any.'
Scarlet said, 'Rose did it, Ruby would never do such a thing.'
Rose said, 'I did it, Scarlet would never be so naughty.'
Violet said, 'It wasn't Rose who spilt the paint, it was Ruby who did it.'
Each of the girls made two statements, one true and one false. *Can you work out which one spilt the paint?*

2. The Cheshire cat is hidden in one of the trees. *From the following clues can you work out the colour of the trunk of the tree it is hidden in?*

(a) The cat is not in a tree with an odd number of branches coming off the trunk.
(b) The cat is hidden in a deciduous tree (one whose leaves fall off in winter).
(c) The cat is not in the tallest tree.
(d) The cat is not in the smallest tree.
(e) The cat's tree would give plenty of shade.

(f) The cat's tree does not bear fruit.
(g) The trunk of the cat's tree is not the widest.

5. 'It'll be off with our heads,' says gardener A to gardener B, 'unless we guess the right colour of the flower under the boot.'
'We can work it out,' says B, ' from the clues given by the other flowers.'
What colour is the flower under the Wellington boot?

6. *Who ate the tarts?* The queen was sitting down and sadly looking at her empty plate.

'I told the boys they could have two tarts each but Indigo,'cos she is small, should have one and then there would be one left for me. Well, when my back was turned the lot were scoffed.
When I asked them, Indigo said, 'I only had one tart, Jack had three.'
Jack said, 'I had no more tarts than Indigo, Jobe only had two tarts.' And Jobe said, 'Indigo ate more than one tart, and Jack only had two.'
'Well, one of them's lying', said the queen.
Can you work out which one was lying?

Here you are at the centre. *Which of the three flowers will you pick?*

Try to make a puzzle path of your own.

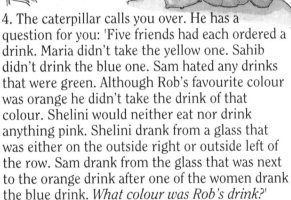

4. The caterpillar calls you over. He has a question for you: 'Five friends had each ordered a drink. Maria didn't take the yellow one. Sahib didn't drink the blue one. Sam hated any drinks that were green. Although Rob's favourite colour was orange he didn't take the drink of that colour. Shelini would neither eat nor drink anything pink. Shelini drank from a glass that was either on the outside right or outside left of the row. Sam drank from the glass that was next to the orange drink after one of the women drank the blue drink. *What colour was Rob's drink?*'

3. The Mad Hatter has painted a cube using the dormouse as a brush. (1) and (2) show all the sides of that coloured cube. *Can you say what the colour is of the side which is face down in (3)?*

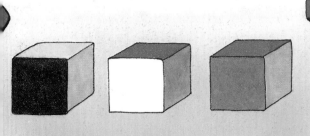

Hedge mazes

The most famous maze in England is to be found in the grounds of Hampton Court Palace. It was laid out for William III in 1690 by two British landscape gardeners called London and Wise. The Hampton Court maze is only about 1000 square metres in area and the longest side is only 68 metres yet the total pathway is over three-quarters of a kilometre long.

There is a rule that might help you to find the way around a maze. Place your right hand against one side of the hedge and follow that edge around. Don't take your hand from the edge. See if the rule works by tracing over the plan of Hampton Court maze. *Do you go down all the pathways?*

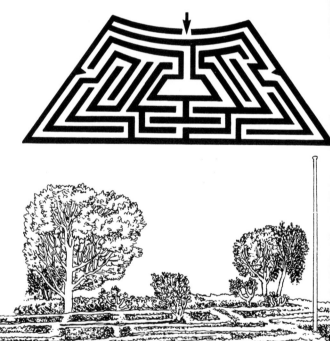

The hedge maze at Blackgang Chine on the Isle of Wight was laid out in 1963.

Unravelling mazes

Does the rule of keeping your right hand on one side of the wall of a maze to be sure of finding your way to the maze centre and out again always work? Check that the right-hand rule works for the maze shown in the diagram here.

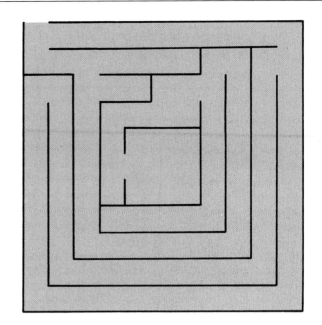

The plan below is of an early version of the maze at Hatfield House in Hertfordshire. Try the right-hand rule.

What happens to you? Why can you never reach the centre? Why do you think that the rule doesn't always work? What is the difference between the first maze and that at Hatfield House?

Is there a method that will get you to the centre and out again for all types of mazes? Can you think of how you would instruct somebody so that he or she would be certain of finding a way to the centre of any maze?

Write down your rules and check to see if they work on the two mazes above.

Terces pot

TELEGRAM

THE SUPPLY OF GAME FOR LONDON IS GOING STEADILY UP HEAD-KEEPER HUDSON WE BELIEVE HAS NOW BEEN TOLD TO RECEIVE ALL ORDERS FOR FLY-PAPER, AND FOR PRESERVATION OF YOUR HEN PHEASANT'S LIFE

The telegram above comes from the beginning of the Sherlock Holmes story, *The Gloria Scott*. It needs to be looked at carefully to decipher the real message which is contained within it. Read the first word and then every following third word of the telegram.

This kind of coded sentence is not easy to create. Try t make up some of your own messages using this rule. Also try to make up some more coded sentences by changing the rule so that you read every fourth, or every fifth word.

Colourful Code

Codes do not have to be made up using letters or numbers... there are many other possibilities. With different combinations of colours for example:

Start with six different colours.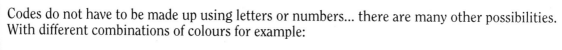

Then use pairs of colours to stand for letters.

So A is   B is   C is

D is   E is   F is

G is   and so on

Can you decode the message in the colourline? You will need to work out the rest of the code above first! Make up some of your own colour codes.

Dancing code

In another story, Sherlock Holmes brings a group of gangsters to justice when he cracks their secret code which uses dancing stick men to stand for letters. The figures below are not the same as the figures which Holmes decoded, but he used the following information and good guesswork to crack the code.

E is the most commonly used letter in written English. After E the letters which are used most often are T, A, O and I – then N, S, H, R and L in that order.

A cracking good code

TIG SRWDVJ OO TIG
HZRRXJTBAN IT
ERWDP TP TIG SVO
OG TIG SRWDVJY
OO TIG OUJHV TXQ
SJFHW

Can you decode the message above? Here are some clues to help your.

1 The first letter of each word is not in code.
2 Right angled triangles of letters are used to put each word into code.
3 The following diagram shows you how to put the word SQUARE into code...

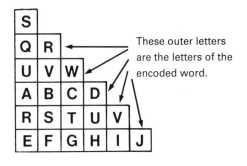

These outer letters are the letters of the encoded word.

Pig pen
The pig pen code was very popular with Union prisoners during the American civil war. *Can you work out the message by using the clue on the right?*

CLUE → ABC|DEF|GHI

105

Problems with primes

What do the numbers 41 and 112 303 have in common? Both are prime numbers. These numbers have fascinated mathematicians ever since their discovery by the Ancient Greeks. The first 20 are shown in this table, which is called a sieve.

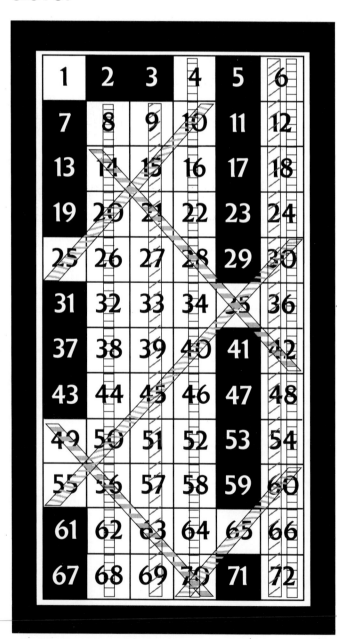

What is a prime number?

A prime number is a number which has exactly two different factors, itself and one. So no other whole number can be divided into it without leaving a remainder. One of the most fascinating things about prime numbers is that they do not appear to form any regular pattern in their occurrence. There is also no easy test which can be used to find out whether a given number is prime or not. It is therefore extremely difficult to find out whether some large numbers are prime.

> 11 is a prime number ...
> 101 is a prime number ...
>
> ... Are 1001 or 10001 prime numbers?

Eratosthenes was a Greek scholar who lived from 276 BC to 194 BC, and was a friend of Archimedes. He pioneered scientific geography and became Head of the Library of Alexandria.

Eratosthenes made a close study of prime numbers, and devised a 'sieve' to find them. Using a table of numbers his method works as follows:

- Cross out all the multiples of 2 except for the number
- Cross out all the multiples of 3 except for the number
- You will find that all the multiples of 4 are already crossed out.
- Cross out all the multiples of 5 except for the number Carry on this method for all the numbers up to the value of the square root of the highest number in the table.
- All the numbers not crossed out are prime.

While there is no predictable pattern for primes there some interesting patterns which hold for a short time. By copying out a number table and colouring in the prime numbers on different-sized grids it is possible to see these patterns.

The highest prime number so far found (in 1992) is $2^{756839} - 1$. It contains 227 832 digits.

Euclid, who lived about 330 BC to 275 BC was a teacher of mathematics in the Museum, in Alexandria. His main contribution to mathematics was to collect all the important work already done by Greek mathematicians into a series of books called the *Elements*.

In the *Elements*, book nine, Euclid covered the theory of number. He wrote a clear and undisputed proof that showed that there is an infinite number of prime numbers.

The proof was by contradiction. Say you thought that that you had the biggest prime number – we'll

The first modern university was founded in Alexandria in 300 BC. It was called the Museum after the Greek goddesses of Arts and Science, the Muses.

call it p. Multiply together all the known smaller primes, including p, and add 1.

$$2 \times 3 \times 5 \times 7 \times ... \times p + 1 = B$$

B cannot be divided by any of the smaller primes so it must therefore be a bigger prime. Thus p cannot be the biggest prime.

ere are also some other questions you could explore. numbers can be made by multiplying prime mbers together ... 24 can be made by $2 \times 2 \times 2 \times 3$. It 4 prime factors. *Which numbers below 100 have the gest number of prime factors?*

o thousand years after Euclid prime numbers still rigued mathematicians. Before computers, testing a - or seven-digit number took weeks of calculation, l many numbers that were thought of as prime were er proved not to be so.

dbach, an 18th century mathematician, suggested t every even number can be made by adding two me numbers together.

    2 is 1 + 1
    4 is 2 + 2
    6 is 3 + 3
    8 is 3 + 5

n *you make all of the even numbers up to 100 like s?* (A list of prime numbers up to 100 would help.)

i will have noticed that Goldbach used 1 as a prime mber. There are arguments about whether 1 can be ught of as prime or not. *What do you think?*

the 19th century it was suggested that every even mber can be made by subtracting two consecutive me numbers in an infinite number of ways. For mple, 6 can be made by subtracting 11 from 17 or 13 m 19.

t using the prime numbers from 1 to 100, can you l out *how many different ways there are of making number 6 by subtracting two consecutive prime*

numbers? It is also possible to make other even numbers, and if you have a larger list of prime numbers you can explore how many different ways you can find for making each even number in this way.

It has also been stated that half of the prime numbers can be made up by adding two square numbers together. For example you can make 5 with $1^2 + 2^2$ and 17 with $1^2 + 4^2$. *Do you think this is true?*

Dudeney puzzles

Henry Ernest Dudeney, a mathematician and author of many mathematical puzzle books, posed the following interesting problem about digits and primes.

You must use each of the 9 digits once and once only. Make a set of prime numbers which will add to the smallest possible total. For example:

$$\begin{array}{r} 61 \\ 283 \\ 47 \\ + 59 \\ \hline 450 \end{array}$$

Is it possible to make a smaller total than this?

Dudeney was also credited with having constructed a 3×3 magic square using the following prime numbers:

1, 7, 13, 31, 37, 43, 61, 67 and 73

If all the horizontal, vertical and diagonal lines have to add up to the same number (the magic constant) what would Dudeney's magic square have been?

Adventure maze

Your ship was wrecked in a violent storm. You find yourself washed ashore on a desert island somewhere in the Pacific.

- If you decide to explore the island go to page 3.

- If you decide to set up a beacon go to page 2.

1

You climb out to a spot high on a cliff looking out to sea. You are building a beacon when you hear a loud noise in the undergrowth behind you.

- If you decide to investigate the noise go to page 4.

- If you decide to go to the beach to get more wood go to page 5.

2

Going along the coastline you discover some large caves sparkling with jewels encrusted in the high rocks of their roofs.

- If you decide to collect some jewels go to page 7.
  If you decide to return to your landing place go to page 6

- If you decide to carry on without going into the cave, go to page 8.

3

Deep in the undergrowth you find yourself following a large bear-like animal along a strangely smooth pathway.

- If you decide to continue along the pathway go to page 12.

- If you decide to turn back go to page 13.

4

You trudge along for what seems an age. Suddenly you see light and run towards it.

- Go to page 2.

9

You find yourself in a huge cavern. Warm water is lapping around you. Looking down you see bright star fish swimming about.

- If you decide to go back towards the light go to page 8.

- If you decide to explore deeper go to page 15.

10

At the far end of the beach you notice a small stream flowing down a hill.

- If you decide to follow the stream to its source go to page 15.

- If you decide to rest and sit on the beach to think about where you are, go to page 16.

11

The pathway leads to a magnificent walled city. Boldly you go through the gates and find yourself trapped there forever!

12

Making up an adventure

You will need to decide how many pages your adventure story is to have. Sixteen is a good number to start with.

The next stage is to make a decision map. The decision map for the desert island story is shown on the right.

Once you have decided on the various possible routes you can start writing your own story. It is best to do i in rough first to make sure it works. Lay out sixteen mini-pages for the whole book on a big sheet.

When you make up your finished story it will be bette to make it as a small booklet so that readers will not b able to look ahead too easily, to see what will happen them if they choose the wrong route! A sixteen-page booklet can be made by folding four sheets of A4 pape in half and stapling them together. If you want to mal less complicated stories use less pages. For more complex stories add pages.

story adventure game is like a maze because you have to thread a way
rough the story by making decisions. Solve the story maze below then
ake your own adventure.

s you climb down the cliff you alise you have taken a wrong ute for the path has led you into idergrowth. If you decide to follow the pathway go to page 12. If you decide to try and get to the beach go to page 14.  **5**	For some reason your brief look into the cave has confused you. You find yourself going further away from your landing place. ● Go to page 8.  **6**

As you go further into the cave it becomes difficult to see. The jewels were an illusion created by bright light reflected from the moist rocks. You come to a forked path in the cave. ● If you go to the right go to page 9. ● If you go to the left go to page 10. **7**	You find yourself in a sheltered bay. A boat is lying tied up on the beach. ● If you decide to take the boat go to page 10. ● If you decide to ignore it go to page 11.  **8**

ou lose your way trying to turn to the beach and find ourself on another part of the land. A cool lagoon beckons ou towards it. Go to page 15.  **3**	Darkness is falling. It has been a long and exhausting day. You find your original shelter and decide to get some rest. ● Go to page 1.  **14**

 You find yourself in a beautiful place. There is a good supply of fresh fruit and water. There are many wonderful fish swimming about in the lagoon. It is so tranquil, you decide to make it your home. **15**	You are sitting on the beach as the sun is setting. Hearing voices call, you look out to sea and there is the rescue boat with other survivors on board. With great joy you are reunited with your friends and sail for home. **16**

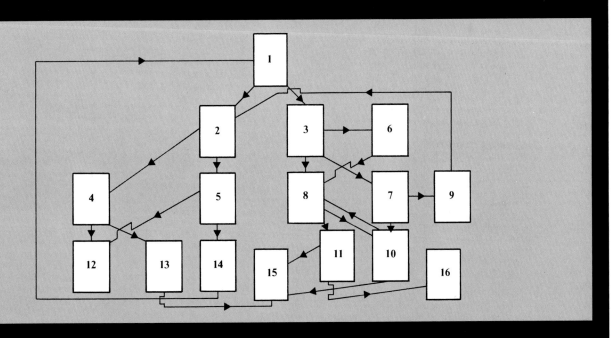

Sets and spots

A double six set of dominos contains 28 pieces. How many dominoes in a double five set...? a double seven set...?

How many spots are there in a double six set of dominoes? A double five set?

Around the edge of this page is an incomplete set of dominoes. Which set is it? Which one is missing?

A double six set of dominoes consists of different tiles, each with a pair of spots, except for the blanks. On the right are the 28 tiles which would make up the double six set. Unfortunately some have been left blank. Can you work out which are missing?

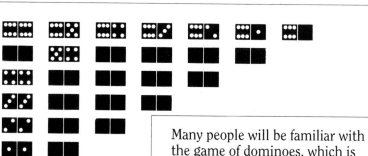

Many people will be familiar with the game of dominoes, which is normally played with a double six set. There are many interesting puzzles which can be explored using the domino pieces.

This group of dominoes consists of all the dominoes from a set whose spots add up to six. Investigate other groups which are made up of spots which add up to other totals.

Here are two groups of dominoes. Each group has a total of eight spots. What is the largest group with a total of ten spots? Investigate different sets of dominoes for different totals of spots.

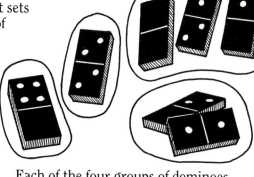

The group of dominoes on the right consists of dominoes where the difference between the half tiles is always 3. Are there any more? Investigate other differences.

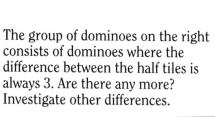

Each of the four groups of dominoes above has 4 spots in it. Each group consists of different dominoes. How many groups are there which add up to 5 spots, 6 spots...? Investigate!

Cards, matches and dice

Cards...

Use the cards from Ace (one) to nine from one suit. Shuffle the cards and lay them out in 3 rows of 3.

By moving one card at a time, rearrange the cards so that they are in descending order from nine to one.

The rules are that you may only move a card from the bottom of a row and it can only be placed on a card of higher value, or into the empty space if you have an empty row.

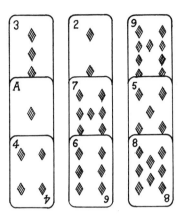

Playing card year

How many spots are there in a pack of cards?

How many cards in a pack?

How many picture cards in a pack?

How many suits?

... matches...

Use 10 matches.

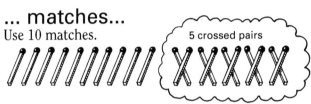

5 crossed pairs

The idea is to move the matches so that they are in pairs.

The rules are that you must jump over exactly two matches when moving. You may only move one match at a time. You don't have to start at the ends and you can move in both directions.

How many different ways can you find for solving the problem?

Use 15 matches.

Move the matches into sets of three. The rules are that you must jump over exactly three matches when moving. You may move only one match at a time.

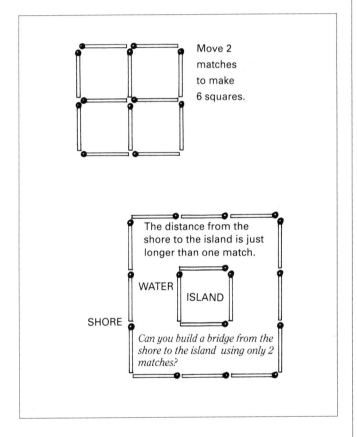

Move 2 matches to make 6 squares.

The distance from the shore to the island is just longer than one match.

WATER   ISLAND

SHORE

Can you build a bridge from the shore to the island using only 2 matches?

... and dice

How many different ways are there of putting the numbers 1 to 6 on a dice?

	6	
4	1	2
	3	
	5	

How many different ways are there of putting the numbers 1 to 6 on the dice if the numbers on opposite sides add up to seven? What do you usually find on a dice?

Puzzling cubes

To solve the Rubik Cube puzzle by trial and error would be a daunting task. There are over 43 000 000 000 000 000 000 possible arrangements of the little cubes.

Rubik's Cube

Perhaps the biggest puzzle craze of this half of the century is that of the Rubik Cube. First developed in Hungary in the 1970s by Erno Rubik, it was in plentiful supply across the world as millions of children and adults twisted it around trying to get the cube back to its original state.

At first glance a Rubik Cube appears to be a simple 3 x x 3 cube with each of the six 3 x 3 outside faces a different colour. But once in your hand you find that the columns and rows can be twisted horizontally or vertically.

To do the Rubik Cube puzzle you first twist columns and rows in a haphazard way until all of the six faces are multicoloured. To solve the puzzle you must return the cube to its original state (i.e. a single colour on each of the six faces). With over 43 000 000 000 000 000 000 possible arrangements this is no easy task. It would be impossible to do it simply by trial and error. The easiest way is to take the cube apart, admire the simple but extremely clever construction that makes the movements of the cube possible and then to replace the parts so that the faces are their original colour.

Colour the cube

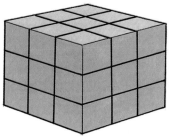

If you put 27 blocks of wood together to make a cube and then paint the outside orange...

How many blocks of wood will have just one side painted orange?
... 2 sides painted orange? ... 3 sides painted orange... 0 sides painted orange?

What if you put 64 blocks together and painted the outside orange?

What about 125 blocks ... 216 ...?

Cube routes

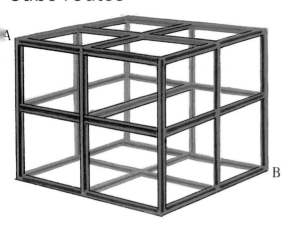

The diagram above represents the skeleton of a building constructed with girders. A construction worker wanted to get from A to B by either walking along horizontal girders or climbing down vertical girders (without going backwards or upwards).
How many possible routes are there?

Report
From Ms. Jones Chief Inspector
I was inspecting the scales of Brown's shop on the main street. I discovered that the shop was using dishonest scales — one arm was longer than the other.
LONGER →

When I put 3 circular weights on the long arm they balance with 8 cube weights on the short arm. When I put one cube on the long arm it balanced six circular weights on the other arm. The true weight of a circular weight is 10 grams.

What is the weight of a cube?

The Soma cube

Can the seven pieces above be fitted together to form a solid 3 x 3 cube? The answer is yes! In fact there are more than 230 different ways - not counting reflections or rotations - to put the cube together. The seven pieces were devised by Piet Hien in Denmark. He originally visualised the puzzle in his mind during a lecture, and later made up a set by sticking wooden blocks together. *How many different ways can you find of making the cube?* The shape below is made using all seven Soma pieces. *Can you construct it?* Devise some shapes of your own.

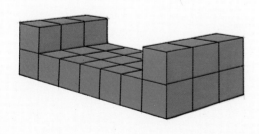

An investigation with cubes

Look at the seven pieces that make up the Soma Cube. One piece is made from three cubes. The other six pieces are made by putting together four cubes. *How many different arrangements are there of five cubes, six cubes...?*

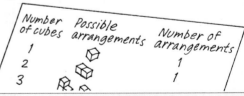

Number of cubes	Possible arrangements	Number of arrangements
1	◇	
2	◇◇	1
3	◇◇ ◇	1

These shapes are made using four cubes. They are mirror images of each other. They are counted as different shapes because it is impossible to turn one over and get the other shape.

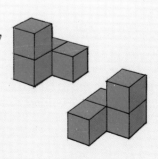

113

On average

The word 'average' comes from an Arabic word meaning damaged goods, which was used by traders in medieval Venice. It was one of the earliest forms of insurance. Groups of merchants who were sending goods by sea would agree that if any particular merchant's goods were damaged or washed overboard the other merchants would club together and thus spread the cost of replacing the lost or damaged goods.

Recent statistics published by an international aid organisation give the average birth rate per woman in the United Kingdom as 1.9 children. *Have you ever come across 0.9 of a child?*

The answer to the question above is obviously 'no'. How was this average arrived at and how is it useful? There are three types of average with each having its own uses. The types are *mean*, *mode* and *median*.

Mean
The mean is found by collecting a set of data, such as the heights of students in a class, adding that data together and then dividing by the number of items, in this example the number of students.

Mode
The mode is found by looking at a set of data and finding which occurs most often.

Median
The median is found by putting a set of data in order of size and finding the middle item. If you have an even number of data and there are two items in the middle, the median is midway between these two.

Class 7R
There are fifteen students in class 7R. Each was measured by the teacher using a metric rule. *Can you find the mean height, the mode height and the median height of the class? Which five pupils are of average height?*

Bob 1.9m · Susie 1.5m · Emily 1.8m · Megan 1.7m · Alexia 1.4m · Lilah 1.4m · Liling 1.5m · Charlie 1.9m · Carmel 1.4m · Dimitri 1.8m · Jose 2m · Ahmed 1.6m · Kim 1.4m · Mamooda 1.3m · Maria 1.7m

On average how long does it take a person to eat a scoop of ice cream?

What is the average number of people sitting at a table?

What is the average number of chairs at a table?

What is the average wait for a banana split if it can take 5 minutes, 7 minutes or 11 minutes – depending on how busy the palour is?

Which ice cream is favourite with the customers?

ORDERS

Table 1
DOUBLE SCOOP OF RASP. AND CHOC. TRIPLE SCOOP OF STRAW, CHOC AND VANILLA

Table 2
SINGLE SCOOP OF CHOC. DOUBLE SCOOP OF RASP. AND B.BERRY. DOUBLE SCOOP OF FUDGE AND CHOC

Table 3
DOUBLE SCOOP OF PIST. AND STRAW. TRIPLE SCOOP OF STRAW, CHOC AND FUDGE

BAR
BANANA SPLIT WITH TWO SCOOPS OF VANILLA

Pay rise

This is a list of the 10 staff and their hourly pay rates at the ice-cream parlour.

Number	Job	Hourly pay
1	Manager	£10
4	Waiter	£5
3	Cook	£3
2	Washer	£2

The owner had agreed that everyone of the staff could have a pay rise of 10% of the average hourly pay.

During a quiet period the cooks each worked out what they thought the hourly rise would be.

IT'LL BE 40p

NO, IT WILL BE 43p

NONSENSE - IT SHOULD BE 50p

Which type of average had each of the cooks used to calculate the rise?

Which average do you think would be fairest? How much would the owner pay?

How much would the owner pay if he just raised each of the hourly rates by 10% instead of finding an average?

Maze games

Making a probability maze game

You will need a coin and coloured counters to play this game.

Toss a coin to decide who starts. Begin from the start position. Each player takes it in turn to flip a coin and move according to the way the coin lands. You only move one space per turn. You may only move along the direction of the arrow, and must go if possible. If you can't move you miss a turn. The first player to reach finish is the winner.

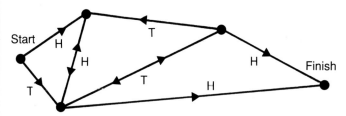

When you have played the game using this board, design your own. Choose the number of landing points, make up rules to decide which paths are heads or tails and in which directions you are allowed to travel.

How could you make the game easier or more difficult? Would some boards be impossible to complete?

Making a mathematical maze

When you solve this maze you will also be able to design similar mazes which are based on mathematical principles.

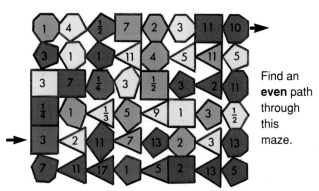

Find an **even** path through this maze.

This is a maze with no obvious path There are three ingredients in it. The colours – red, yellow, blue, green – represent the numbers 1, 2, 3 and 4 but not necessarily in that order. The product of all three ingredients, when correctly combined, are all whole numbers and will give the only even pathway from start to finish.

Busy bees

The game is for two to four players. You will need counters or cut-out 'bees' for each player, the object being to collect pollen from each of the six flowers around the board. Four coloured tokens or cards need to be placed on each flower to represent the pollen.

Players throw two dice to determine who starts first, the highest scorer beginning by placing a bee on the hive in the centre. Bees move around the board by throwing the two dice. The bee may go into the next cell when the number on either of the dice is the same as that on one of the openings. If both numbers are available the bee may choose the order to use them, and move two cells. The numbers must be used, even if it takes the bee in the wrong direction. If neither number corresponds, the bee misses a turn. A bee may not enter a cell already occupied.

To reach a flower the bee must get to one of the cells on the edge of the board, and throw the appropriate number on the dice to go through an opening. It cannot land on a flower if a bee is already there, and should not visit the same flower twice.

Once on the flower, a pollen token is collected. The bee waits until its next turn, then flies straight back to the hive in the centre, providing it is free. The dice are then thrown to begin the journey to a new flower.

If an unlucky throw of the dice forces the bee to return to a flower it has already visited, it must return that flower's pollen, and go back to the hive next turn to start again.

The winner is the bee who collects all six pollen tokens first.

These are not the rules of the original game; you could try variations of these rules, like having only one pollen counter on each flower, and the winner being the first bee to collect three or making it harder to leave the flower by having to throw the dice and trace the way back through the cells. Investigate which rules make the most interesting game.

More puzzling mazes

The house of mazes

Jodie has found instructions to help her find treasure hidden somewhere in a maze of rooms of a deserted house. The problem is that there are three floors and she does not know which one the instructions have been written for. *Can you tell on which floor she should search, and then where the treasure is hidden?*

Enter the maze of rooms through the open doorway. Go through the doorway opposite you in the first room. When you are in the next room turn right and walk through the doorway. Then take the doorway on your left. Go through the doorway on your left again and then go straight ahead through another doorway. When you have gone through the doorway on your left you will find the treasure.

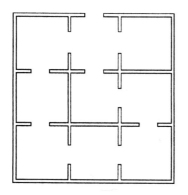
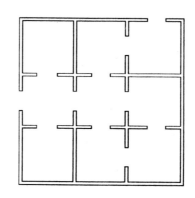
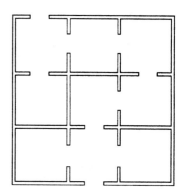

Instructions for a robot

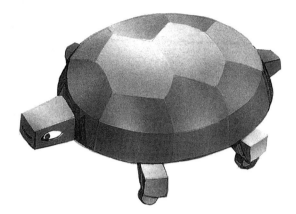

Working out a set of instructions to guide someone through a maze may be quite complicated, but it would be especially important to be accurate for a robot turtle which could only do as it had been instructed and could not make choices itself. Write a set of instructions for a robot turtle so that it could happily find its way in and out of these simple mazes.

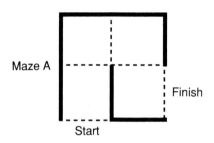

Maze A

Finish

Start

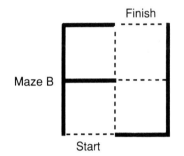

Finish

Maze B

Start

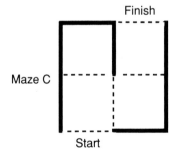

Finish

Maze C

Start

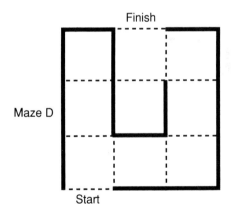

Finish

Maze D

Start

You will need to think carefully about the instructions. You can assume that the robot turtle would be able to understand that 'Move' meant 'a forward move from one square into the next'. Other useful instructions could be:

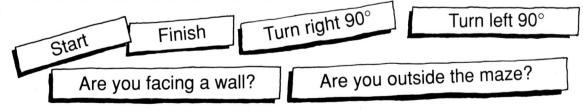

Start   Finish   Turn right 90°   Turn left 90°

Are you facing a wall?   Are you outside the maze?

See if your set of instructions works on other sizes of maze.

The path to infinity

In school the students are having an infinitely long day. They are finding it difficult to come to terms with the idea that the Universe goes on forever outwards as well as inwards. At the same time they are trying to grasp that they can never find either the largest or the smallest number. One student thinks he has found the biggest number, another adds one. If a student finds the smallest number then someone else divides it by ten.

Suppose there are an infinite number of students in school today. The first lesson is geography and every student is given a geography exercise book. It is then decided that all of the pupils will now study mathematics and art as well, so two further exercise books are given to each pupil. *How many books will be needed now?*

The infinite number of pupils in Infinity School have numbers on their backs. The teacher asks the infinite number of pupils to join hands with the person who has one more than their number on their back. The teacher then changes the rule and asks all of the pupils to join hands with the person who has the number which is three more than them on their back. *How many pupils end up playing in the second game?*

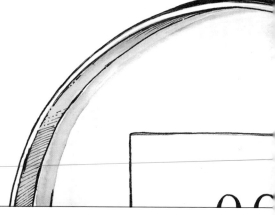

ch mirror image is half the size of the previous one.
*all the mirror images were stacked on top of each
her how tall would they be in relation to the full size
ure?*

In the mathematics
classroom the
pupils are looking
for the smallest
number. *Will they
ever find it?*

0.5   1

0.05

0.005

0.0005

0.00005

05

A few solutions

Page 4 **Names for numbers**
Finger 1, Eyes 2, Feyes 3, Limbs 4, Flimbs 5, Elimbs 6,
Feyelimbs 7, Limblimbs 8, Flimblimbs 9, Flimbflimbs 10

Page 5 **Pounds, shillings and pence**
£14/5/6d (Fourteen pounds, five shillings and sixpence)
£10/18/3d (Ten pounds, eighteen shillings and threepence)
£29/19/3d (Twenty-nine pounds, nineteen shillings and threepence)
£3/9/6d (Three pounds, nine shillings and sixpence)

Page 7 **Problem 79**
$7^5 = 16\,807$ measures of flour
PS to problem 79
One!

Page 12 **Cabbages, goat and wolf**

  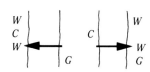

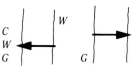 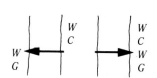

Mothers and daughters
5 journeys

Jealous husbands
5 journeys

Page 13 **More jealous husbands**
9 journeys

Page 14 **Zero sums**

$100 + 0 = 100$	$100 \div 0 = \infty$	$0 \times 100 = 0$
$0 - 100 = -100$	$0 + 100 = 100$	$0 \div 100 = 0$
$100 \times 0 = 0$	$100 - 0 = 100$	

Page 15 **On the cards**
The following are all the 2-digit numbers in the Fibonacci series:
13, 21, 34, 55, 89. The number 13 is prime because it has exactly
two distinct factors: 1 and 13.
$13 \times 13 = 169$, which is a 3-digit number.
(89 is also prime, but its square is a 4-digit number, 7921.)

Page 16 **Eggs**
Mrs Holly started out with 63 eggs.

Page 17 **Sacks**
A weighs 5.5 kg, B weighs 6.5 kg, C weighs 7 kg,
D weighs 4.5 kg, E weighs 3.5 kg.

Page 18 **Horse puzzle**

Pie
22 pieces

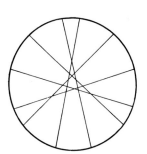

Nine eggs
4 connected lines

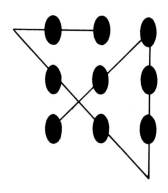

Page 19 **The Merchant's puzzle**
7560

Dividing three numbers
79

The dispatch rider
$106 \frac{2}{3}$ miles

Page 22 **Moving crates**
It can be done in less than 22 moves.

Moving pyramids
It can be done in 5 moves.

Page 23 **Sliding cups and saucers**
It can be done in less than 47 moves.

Strang interview
It can be done in less than 18 moves.

Page 24 **How many grains?**
25 000 000 000 000 (If 20 grains of sand equal a grain of wheat
and 125 grains of wheat make a cubic centimetre.)

Page 25 **Sky high numbers**
Mercury: 5.8×10^7; Venus: 1.1×10^8; Jupiter: 7.7×10^8;
Saturn: 1.4×10^9; Uranus: 2.8×10^9; Neptune: 4.4×10^9;
Pluto: 5.9×10^9; Altair: 1.5×10^{14}; Sirius: 8.2×10^{13};
Procyon: 1.04×10^{14}; Beta Centauri: 3.7×10^{15}.

Page 26 **Which base?**
First: base 4; Second: base 2; Third: base 3; Fourth: base 5

Page 27 **Base two additions**
11101, 1010001, 100110, 10000110

Base two subtractions
100, 1100, 10010, 1001

New job

12.05   16 + 4 = 20
12.10   80 + 20 = 100
12.15 400 + 100 = 500
.
.
.
1.00 976 562 500

Doubling

$\frac{1}{32\,768}$

Page 28 **Silver and sisters**
2 shekels 36 grains

Babylonian square
The side of the square is 30 units.

Page 29 **Measuring land**

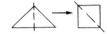

The other two are quite difficult. Look at the shape that they
finish up as. Try to imagine how the original shape could be cut
up to make them. (They each require 2 cuts.)

Babylonian hand
Length = 6, width = 4

Page 31 **Pig in the garden**

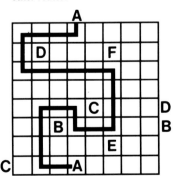

Cat and mice
The minimum number of moves is 12.

Tower of London
The diagram shows the route of A. Can you now work out the
other routes?

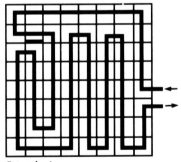

Page 32 **How many squares on a chessboard?**
204 squares

Page 33 **Lions and crowns**
This is one of the four identical shapes.
Can you work out how they fit together
and where the crowns and lions go?

The golden chessboard
This is one of the four identical shapes.
Can you work out how they fit together
and where the jewels go?

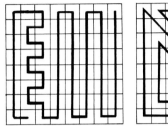

Page 34 **Routes**

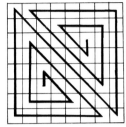

Page 35 **24 ounces**
It can be done with 7 pourings

4 litres

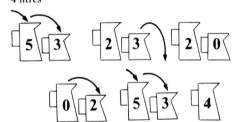

Page 36 **Consecutive numbers for m and n**

when $m = 2$ and $n = 1$ $m^2 - n^2 = 3$ $2mn = 4$ $m^2 + n^2 = 5$
when $m = 3$ and $n = 2$ $m^2 - n^2 = 5$ $2mn = 12$ $m^2 + n^2 = 13$
when $m = 4$ and $n = 3$ $m^2 - n^2 = 7$ $2mn = 24$ $m^2 + n^2 = 25$
when $m = 5$ and $n = 4$ $m^2 - n^2 = 9$ $2mn = 40$ $m^2 + n^2 = 41$

Triangle numbers for m and n
Here are the first few triangle numbers: 1, 3, 6, 10, 15, 21 and 28.

when $m = 3$ and $n = 1$ $m^2 - n^2 = 8 = 2 \times 4$ $2mn = 6 = 2 \times 3$
                                $m^2 + n^2 = 10 = 2 \times 5$
when $m = 6$ and $n = 3$ $m^2 - n^2 = 27 = 3 \times 9$ $2mn = 36 = 3 \times 12$
                                $m^2 + n^2 = 45 = 3 \times 15$
when $m = 10$ and $n = 6$ $m^2 - n^2 = 64 = 4 \times 16$ $2mn = 120 = 4 \times 30$
                                $m^2 + n^2 = 136 = 4 \times 34$

Page 37 **Square to square**

Perigal's dissection

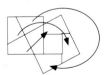

Triangles to spirals

Page 38 Abacus
Chinese: 123 456 789; Russian: 7 483 621 954;
Japanese: 7946.872 345 769 4

Page 39 A number puzzle
Here are three ways:

```
3 4 1   3 8 1   2 7 3
5 8 6   6 5 4   5 4 6
9 2 7   9 7 2   8 1 9
```

Page 42 Perfect numbers
496 and 8128

Imperfect numbers
Deficient: 35 (sum of factors 13), 42 (sum of factors 41),
64 (sum of factors 63), 99 (sum of factors 57), 155 (sum of
factors 37)
Abundant: 56 (sum of factors 64), 70 (sum of factors 74),
84 (sum of factors 140), 102 (sum of factors 136)

Page 43 Attica symbols
Top left: 22 284; top right: 3142; bottom left: 17 296;
bottom right 18 416

Ancient Greek puzzle
120 olives

Ionic numbers

Page 46 Topological trick 1

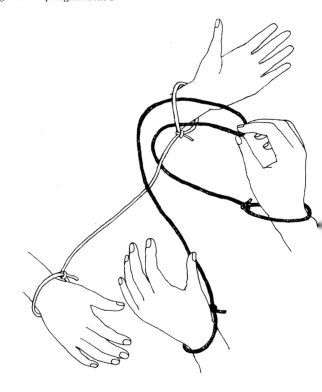

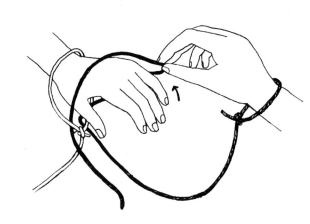

Page 49 Ways in ways out
The prime numbers go through 7, 8, 9 or 10 hexagons.
The multiples of 3 go through 7, 8 or 9 hexagons.
The triangle numbers go through 8 or 9 hexagons.

Rogue dice maze
Here is a net of a dice.
Try to visualise it made up.
What do the opposite
pairs of sides add up to?
Have another look at the
dice maze.

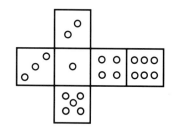

Page 50 The Arrow
Time is continuous and moving just as the arrow is moving. A
particular instant in time passes and cannot be recaptured. So
even if an arrow is stationary it is moving through time! In this
case it is better to think of the arrow moving through the air
and not to consider the time element.

Page 51 **The life of Diophantus**
Diophantus lived to the age of 84 years.

A farmer goes to market
5 cows, 1 pig and 94 sheep

Page 55 **Some puzzling circles**
Floating island   Magic circle

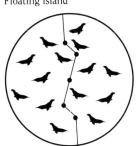 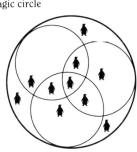

Page 59 **Added to 3**
$x = 4$

Four times
$x = 4$

Seven times
$x = 5$

How old?
Mother is 36 years old, elder daughter is 12 and younger daughter is 2.

Mother and son
Mother is 50 years old and son is 30.

Red and green
36 red, 12 green

Differ by one
8:10

20 more
9 x 20

Page 61 **Spy lights**
471

Page 63 **Knots and unknots**
The knot has been unknotted. Can you work out which two crossings have changed? Make the knot up with string (use tape to hold the crossings in place) and check that it works. Make up some puzzles of your own using real string.

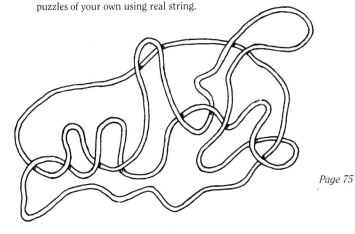

Pages 64-65 **The mathematical mansion**
Look at the drawings below. What is the connection? Check your route and make sure you have got all the right connections.

Pieces   Sides
            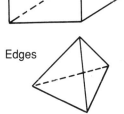

Pieces

                                Edges

Page 68 **Pyramids**
1 crystal would make a square-based pyramid and 4900 would also make a square-based pyramid. 1 crystal would make a triangle-based pyramid and so would 4.

Cube statues
There are 27 cubes in a size 3 cube. There are 1000 cubes in a size 10 cube. If the shape was hollow, a size 3 cube would contain 26 small cubes and a size 10 cube would contain 488.

Page 69 **Windows**
The proportions tend to approximately 0.393 red, 0.607 blue.

Turret roofs
Square numbers on each side:
Tenth turret has $4 \times 10^2 = 400$ tiles.

Path
Fibonacci numbers: 5-tile pavement has 8 arrangements, 6-tile has 13.

Garden
Figurative numbers (triangle, square, ...)

Flags
$\frac{11}{32}$ of the sixth flag will be red.

Page 73 **Colourful doors**
Blue

Page 74 **Cryptarithms**
BAG x GAB B = 2, A = 3, G = 4
ABC x DE A = 1, B= 2, C = 5, D = 3, E = 7
4539281706 x 2 (Are there any other answers?)
SEND + MORE S = 9, E = 5, N= 6, D = 7, M = 1, O = 0, R = 8, Y = 2
TEN + TEN + FORTY = SIXTY T = 8, E = 5, N = 0, F = 2, O = 9, R = 7, Y = 6, S = 3, I = 1, X = 4
WRONG + WRONG = RIGHT One solution is: W = 2, R = 5, O = 9, N = 3, G =8, I = 1, H = 7, T = 6
SEAM x T = MEATS S = 4, E = 9, A = 7, M = 3, T = 8
GREEN x RED = ORANGE G = 4, R = 7, E = 0, N = 5, D = 8, O = 2, A = 9

Page 75 **Arranging numbers**
Circle puzzle: puts 10 in the middle.
Square puzzle: top line is $9 - 5 = 4$.
Triangle puzzle: 1, 5 and 9 could be in the corners.

Page 76   Making numbers

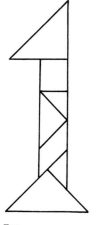

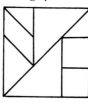

Missing square

Page 77   Eggram

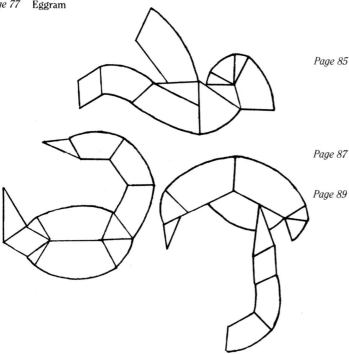

Page 79   An elephant eating buns

Are there other ways?

Page 80   **The Mathematician's Tale**
10! = 3 628 800

Page 81   **Eating out**
7 August

Alphabet
26! = 4.032 914 611 × 10²⁶

Arranging fences

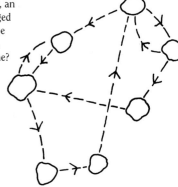

Page 83   **Moving engines**
Engine 5 does not move.
7, 6, 3, 7, 6, 1, 2, 4, 1, 3, 8, 1, 3, 2, 4, 3, 2

The white bishop
The fewest number of moves is 17.

Page 85   **A few keys**
All numbers between 1 and 50 can be made using only the six keys shown.

Taxing island
50 000 Nazricks

Page 87   **Reversing**
1. The counters can be reversed in 17 moves.

Page 89   **Delivering supplies**
Map 1 is wrong. Here, an arrow has been changed so that the map can be successfully travelled. Can you see which one?

Page 91   **Talisman Square**
Every difference between any numbers next door to each other is greater than 2.
(There are other solutions.)

13	3	16	5
10	7	11	2
14	1	15	8
6	9	4	12

Page 92   **Pattern windows**
Building on left: 1, 3, 5, . . .; 3, 6, 9, . . .; 1, 2, 4, 7, 11, . . .
Building in centre: half, third, quarter ; Fibonacci numbers; three sides, four sides, five sides, . . .
Building on right: if even halve, if odd multiply by 5 and add 1; prime numbers

Page 93   **Exploring rules**
The first two patterns are made using the following rule: add the two previous digits and put down the units digit as the next number. The next two patterns are: add the two previous digits in base 5 and put down the units digit of the answer as the next number; add the two previous digits in base 7 and put down the units digit of the answer as the next number.

126

Building upwards
For each triangle there is a way of working out what each row will add up to and then it will be possible to find a pattern for each triangle.

1 = 1
11 = 2
111 = 3

Page 97 **Mayan numbers**
(From left to right) 1081, 83 585, 422, 878, 9723

Page 98 **Discs**

Five hats
Yellow

Page 99 **Who got what?**
Alan, 9 years, paint box
Betty, 8 years, felt-tipped pens
Charlie, 7 years, felt-tipped pens
D (not named), 5 years, paint box
Ellen, 10 years, colouring pencils
Fred, 6 years, colouring pencils
(If D is a boy, then D could be 6 years old with colouring pencils and Fred could be 5 years with a paint box.)

Pages 100-101 **Puzzle your way in**
The puzzle's centre: the flower on the right is the correct one. If you can see why, you will be over the rainbow!

Page 103 **Unravelling mazes**
A method for solving all mazes: you can record what you are doing on paper as you walk around the maze and you may need to find a way of marking the maze to show where you have been. The method you find is not likely to give you the shortest route.

Page 104 **Telegram message**
THE GAME IS UP HUDSON HAS TOLD ALL FLY FOR YOUR LIFE

Colourful code
THIS IS AN INTERESTING BECAUSE IT IS MORE LIKE A PATTERN

Page 105 **Dancing code**
Remember that there needs to be a figure for the breaks between words.

Pig pen
ESCAPE TONIGHT

Page 106 **What is a prime number?**
1001 is not a prime number because 143 × 7 = 1001. 10 001 is not a prime number because 137 × 73 = 10 001.

Page 107 **Most prime factors**
2 × 2 × 2 × 2 × 2 × 2 = 64; 2 × 2 × 2 × 2 × 2 × 3 = 96

Making six
There are 11 different ways: 89 – 83, 79 – 73, 67 – 61, 59 – 53, 53 – 47, 37 – 31, 29 – 23, 23 – 17, 19 – 13, 17 – 11 and 11 – 5

Dudeney puzzles
2 + 47 + 59 + 61 + 83; 111

Page 110 **Missing domino**
The double blank is missing.

Page 111 **. . . Matches . . .**
Here is one solution. Number matches 1 to 10 and then move as follows: 5 to pair with 2, 7 to 10, 3 to 8, 9 to 6 and 4 to 1.

6 squares **Island**

Page 113 **Cube routes**
Start with a 1 × 1 × 1 cube. How many routes are there?

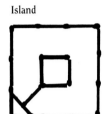

Cubes
Cube weight 15 grams

Page 114 **Class 7R**
Mean: 1.62 m; mode: 1.4 m; median: 1.6 m
Alexia, Carmel, Kim, Lilah (mode)
Ahmed (median)

Pages 114-115 **The average ice-cream parlour**
Eating a scoop of ice cream: It is difficult to answer this question as no data is given. You could buy an ice cream and time yourself eating it. You could get your friends to do the same. Would you have a good average? Do young people eat ice cream faster than older people? Just how big is a scoop of ice cream?

Page 115 **Pay rise**
Median: 40p; mean: 43p; mode 50p

Page 116 **A mathematical maze**
Below is one of the columns of the maze which shows the product of the three ingredients. Which column is it? Can you solve the maze now?
51 55 3 7 5 10

Page 118 **The house of mazes**
The floor plan on the right

Page 121 **Mirror images**
Height of all mirror images on top of each other would be equal to the height of the full-size figure.

A page of numbers

Arabic (Gobar)	Arabic (Modern)	Babylonian	Chinese (Rod)	Chinese	Egyptian (Hieroglyphics)	Egyptian (Hieratic)	Greek (Attic)	Greek (Ionian)	Hebrew	Hindu (Gwalior)	International (modern)	Mayan	Roman
1	١	▼	│	一	∣		∣	A	א		1	·	I
2	٢	▼▼	∥	二	∥		∥	B	ב		2	··	II
3	٣	▼▼▼	∥∣	三	∥∣		∥∣	Γ	ג		3	···	III
4	٤		∥∥	四	∥∥		∥∥	Δ	ד		4	····	IV
5	٥		∥∥∣	五	∥∥∣		Γ	E	ה		5	—	V
6	٦		⊤	六	∥∥∣		ΓΙ	F	ו		6	·	VI
7	٧		⊤⊤	七			ΓΙΙ	Z	ז		7	··	VII
8	٨		⊤⊤⊤	八			ΓΙΙΙ	H	ח		8	···	VIII
9	٩			九			ΓΙΙΙΙ	Θ	ט		9	····	IX
10	١٠	‹	—	十	∩	Λ	Δ	I	י		10	=	X
20	٢٠	‹‹	=	二十	∩∩		ΔΔ	K	כ		20	👁	XX
30	٣٠	‹‹‹	≡	三十	∩∩∩		ΔΔΔ	Λ	ל		30		XXX
40	٤٠		≣	四十	∩∩∩∩		ΔΔΔΔ	M	מ		40	👁	XL
50	٥٠			五十			⌐	N	נ		50		L
60	٦٠	▼	⊥	六十			⌐Δ	Ξ	ס		60		LX
70	٧٠		⊥	七十			⌐ΔΔ	O	ע		70		LXX
80	٨٠		⊥	八十			⌐ΔΔΔ	Π	פ		80		LXXX
90	٩٠		⊥	九十			⌐ΔΔΔΔ	ϙ	צ		90		XC
100	١٠٠		│	百			H	P	ק		100	👁	C
200	٢٠٠		∥	二百			HH	Σ	ר		200		CC
300	٣٠٠		∥∣	三百			HHH	T	ש		300		CCC
400	٤٠٠		∥∥	四百			HHHH	Y	ת		400		CD
500	٥٠٠		∥∥∣	五百			Γᴴ	Φ	ך		500		D
600	٦٠٠	‹	⊤	六百			ΓᴴH	X	ם		600		DC
700	٧٠٠		⊤⊤	七百			ΓᴴHH	Ψ	ן		700		DCC
800	٨٠٠		⊤⊤⊤	八百			ΓᴴHHH	Ω	ף		800		DCCC
900	٩٠٠			九百			ΓᴴHHHH	ↄ	ץ		900		CM

128